Real Estate Development and Deal Making

Essential Guide for Property Developers, Entrepreneurs and Deal Makers

By Willem Tait

Published by WRT Publishing

Copyright © 2024 by Willem Tait
All rights reserved.

No part of this publication may be reproduced, distributed, or transmitted in any form or by any means, including photocopying, recording, or other electronic or mechanical methods, without the prior written permission of the author, except in the case of brief quotations embodied in reviews and certain other noncommercial uses permitted by copyright law.

For permission requests, contact the author at: willemtait@gmail.com

This book is for educational and informational purposes only. The author is not liable for any damages or losses arising from the use or misuse of the content in this book.

Cover Design: Time Brands
Published by WRT Publishing

First Edition

Library ISBN Ebook: 978-0-6398578-3-1
Library ISBN Print: 978-0-6398578-2-4
KDP Amazon Paperback ISBN: 9798302542038
KDP Amazon Hardcover ISBN: 9798302549396

INTRODUCTION

Welcome to *Real Estate Development and Deal Making: The Essential Guide for Property Developers, Entrepreneurs, and Dealmakers*. Whether you're a seasoned developer, an aspiring entrepreneur, or a savvy dealmaker looking to make your mark in the dynamic world of real estate, this book is your roadmap to success.

Real estate development is not just about constructing buildings; it's about envisioning opportunities, creating value, and transforming landscapes into thriving communities. Imagine the power of taking an empty plot of land and turning it into a bustling neighborhood or a profitable investment. This book brings that vision to life, offering you the tools, insights, and strategies you need to bring your ideas from concept to completion.

Inside, you'll find a comprehensive breakdown of the real estate development process, from Market Research and Analysis to Feasibility Studies, and from Financial Planning and Budgeting to Sustainability and Green Development. You'll explore the intricacies of Project Management, the critical role of Legal and Regulatory Considerations, and the exciting potential of Technology and Innovation in reshaping how developments are planned and executed. Each chapter is packed with actionable insights and real-world examples to help you anticipate challenges and seize opportunities.

But this isn't just a book about processes and strategies; it's about inspiration. Throughout, you'll discover case studies of successful projects that demonstrate how vision, creativity, and determination can turn obstacles into steppingstones. Whether you're negotiating deals, navigating risks, or marketing properties, this guide equips you with the knowledge and confidence to make informed decisions and achieve remarkable results.

Turn the page, and let's begin a journey through the art and science of real estate development. Your blueprint for success starts here.

TABLE OF CONTENT

INTRODUCTION 2
TABLE OF CONTENT 4
CHAPTER 1: INTRODUCTION TO PROPERTY
DEVELOPMENT 12
    THE FOUNDATIONS OF PROPERTY
    DEVELOPMENT 13
    PROPERTY DEVELOPMENT AND
    URBANIZATION 14
    THE ROLE OF DEVELOPERS IN PROPERTY
    DEVELOPMENT 15
    ARCHITECTS AND THEIR CONTRIBUTION TO
    DEVELOPMENT 16
    INVESTORS: THE BACKBONE OF PROPERTY
    DEVELOPMENT 17
    CHALLENGES AND OPPORTUNITIES IN
    PROPERTY DEVELOPMENT 17
    THE FUTURE OF PROPERTY DEVELOPMENT .. 18
    LAYING THE GROUNDWORK FOR SUCCESS ... 19
    THE ROAD AHEAD 20
CHAPTER 2: MARKET RESEARCH AND ANALYSIS 21
    UNDERSTANDING THE PROPERTY MARKET ... 21
    IDENTIFYING PROFITABLE LOCATIONS 22
    UNDERSTANDING DEMOGRAPHIC NEEDS 23
    VALUATION AND DEMAND ANALYSIS 23
    TREND FORECASTING AND THE FUTURE OF
    MARKETS 24
    TOOLS FOR EFFECTIVE MARKET RESEARCH . 24
    NAVIGATING MARKET CHALLENGES 25
    THE ROAD AHEAD 26

- CHAPTER 3: FEASIBILITY STUDIES 27
  - THE PURPOSE OF FEASIBILITY STUDIES 27
  - COST ANALYSIS: THE FOUNDATION OF FEASIBILITY 28
  - Types of Costs to Consider: 28
  - MARKET DEMAND: ALIGNING PROJECTS WITH NEEDS 29
  - Key Factors to Assess: 29
  - LOCATION BENEFITS: THE IMPORTANCE OF SITE ANALYSIS 30
  - Components of Site Analysis: 30
  - RETURN ON INVESTMENT (ROI): MEASURING PROFITABILITY 31
  - Calculating ROI: 31
  - COSTINGS AND BUDGETING: STAYING ON TRACK 32
  - Tips for Effective Costings: 32
  - POTENTIAL UPSIDE: IDENTIFYING OPPORTUNITIES 32
  - Examples of Potential Upsides: 32
  - NAVIGATING CHALLENGES THROUGH FEASIBILITY 33
  - THE ROAD AHEAD 34
- CHAPTER 4: FINANCIAL PLANNING AND BUDGETING 35
  - THE IMPORTANCE OF FINANCIAL STRATEGIES 36
  - PROJECT FUNDING: SOURCES AND STRATEGIES 37
  - Common Sources of Project Funding: 37
  - BUDGETING: CREATING A ROADMAP FOR SUCCESS 38
  - Key Components of a Development Budget: 38

COST CONTROL: MANAGING EXPENSES EFFECTIVELY 39
Strategies for Cost Control: 39
MAXIMIZING PROFITABILITY 40
Factors That Influence Profitability: 41
INVESTMENT STRATEGIES: BUILDING LONG-TERM SUCCESS 41
Principles of Investment in Property Development: 41
THE ROAD AHEAD 43
CHAPTER 5: PROJECT MANAGEMENT 44
THE ROLE OF PROJECT MANAGEMENT IN REAL ESTATE DEVELOPMENT 45
SCHEDULING: BUILDING THE FOUNDATION FOR SUCCESS 46
Key Elements of Effective Scheduling: 46
WORKFLOW: STREAMLINING THE DEVELOPMENT PROCESS 47
Components of Effective Workflow Management: .. 47
RESOURCE ALLOCATION: MAXIMIZING EFFICIENCY 48
Strategies for Effective Resource Allocation: 48
COORDINATION: BRINGING STAKEHOLDERS TOGETHER 49
Best Practices for Stakeholder Coordination: 49
MEETING DEADLINES: DELIVERING ON TIME .. 50
Strategies for Meeting Deadlines: 50
THE ROAD AHEAD 51
CHAPTER 6: LEGAL AND REGULATORY CONSIDERATIONS 52
COMPLIANCE: THE CORNERSTONE OF SUCCESS 53
Key Areas of Compliance in Property Development:

....53
- ZONING: DEFINING LAND USE..........................54
- Common Zoning Classifications: 54
- BUILDING CODES: ENSURING SAFETY AND QUALITY 55
- Key Aspects of Building Codes:................................55
- PERMITS: NAVIGATING THE APPROVAL PROCESS 56
- CONTRACTS: BUILDING TRUST AND CLARITY.57
- Key Elements of Effective Contracts: 57
- RISK MANAGEMENT THROUGH LEGAL COMPLIANCE 58
- Strategies for Risk Management: 58
- THE ROAD AHEAD..59

CHAPTER 7: CONSTRUCTION AND DEVELOPMENT PROCESS 60
- SITE PREPARATION: LAYING THE GROUNDWORK..61
- Key Steps in Site Preparation:.................................61
- DESIGN AND PLANNING: TURNING IDEAS INTO BLUEPRINTS 62
- Key Elements of the Design Phase: 62
- MATERIALS AND SUPPLY CHAIN: BUILDING BLOCKS OF SUCCESS..63
- Key Considerations for Material Management:........63
- CONSTRUCTION MANAGEMENT: BRINGING THE PROJECT TO LIFE 64
- Key Components of Construction Management:.....64
- INSPECTION AND QUALITY ASSURANCE: DELIVERING EXCELLENCE 65
- Key Steps in Inspection and Quality Assurance:.....65
- THE PERSPECTIVES OF DEVELOPERS,

ENTREPRENEURS, AND DEALMAKERS 66
THE ROAD AHEAD 67
CHAPTER 8: MARKETING AND SALES STRATEGIES 68
POSITIONING PROPERTIES: BUILDING A BRAND 69
Key Steps in Property Positioning: 69
PRE-SELLING AND PRE-LETTING: CREATING EARLY MOMENTUM 70
Benefits of Pre-Selling and Pre-Letting:..................70
Strategies for Pre-Selling and Pre-Letting: 70
MARKETING DURING CONSTRUCTION: MAINTAINING INTEREST 71
Best Practices for Marketing During Construction:..71
POST-COMPLETION MARKETING: MAXIMIZING VALUE 72
Post-Completion Strategies: 72
SALES STRATEGIES: CLOSING THE DEAL........73
Key Sales Techniques: 73
INSIGHTS FROM MY BOOKS 74
THE ROAD AHEAD 75
CHAPTER 9: RISK MANAGEMENT 76
UNDERSTANDING RISK: A FOUNDATION FOR SUCCESS 76
Types of Risks in Real Estate:................................77
THE PROPERTY DEVELOPER'S PERSPECTIVE 77
Key Risks for Developers: 77
Mitigation Strategies for Developers:......................78
THE ENTREPRENEUR'S PERSPECTIVE 79
Key Risks for Entrepreneurs:...................................79
Mitigation Strategies for Entrepreneurs: 79

THE DEALMAKER'S PERSPECTIVE 80
Key Risks for Dealmakers: 80
Mitigation Strategies for Dealmakers: 80
CAPITAL MARKETS AND RISK MANAGEMENT..81
STRATEGIES FOR EFFECTIVE RISK
MANAGEMENT 82
Universal Risk Management Strategies: 82
THE ROAD AHEAD 83
CHAPTER 10: SUSTAINABILITY AND GREEN
DEVELOPMENT 84
THE SHIFT TOWARD SUSTAINABILITY IN REAL
ESTATE 85
Key Drivers of Sustainability: 85
GREEN BUILDING AND ECO-FRIENDLY
CONSTRUCTION 86
Key Features of Green Buildings: 86
THE BUSINESS CASE FOR SUSTAINABILITY 87
Benefits of Sustainability: 87
NEGOTIATING GREEN DEALS: A WIN-WIN
APPROACH 88
Strategies for Negotiating Green Deals: 88
THE ENTREPRENEUR'S ROLE IN GREEN
DEVELOPMENT 88
Opportunities for Entrepreneurs: 89
DEVELOPERS AND SUSTAINABILITY: TURNING
VISION INTO REALITY 89
Key Steps for Developers: 89
REAL ESTATE ECONOMICS AND
SUSTAINABILITY 90
THE ROAD AHEAD 91
CHAPTER 11: TECHNOLOGY AND INNOVATION IN
PROPERTY DEVELOPMENT 92

9

THE RISE OF PROPTECH: THE FUTURE OF REAL ESTATE 93
Key Applications of PropTech: 93
ARTIFICIAL INTELLIGENCE: ENHANCING DECISION-MAKING 94
Key Applications of AI in Real Estate: 94
3D MODELING AND VIRTUAL REALITY: BRINGING PROJECTS TO LIFE 95
Applications of 3D Modeling and VR: 95
SMART BUILDING SYSTEMS: THE FUTURE OF PROPERTY MANAGEMENT 96
Features of Smart Building Systems: 96
THE DEALMAKER'S ADVANTAGE: LEVERAGING TECHNOLOGY IN NEGOTIATIONS 97
How Dealmakers Use Technology: 97
THE ENTREPRENEUR'S EDGE: INNOVATING WITH TECHNOLOGY 98
Opportunities for Entrepreneurs: 98
THE DEVELOPER'S PERSPECTIVE: BUILDING WITH INNOVATION 99
How Developers Use Technology: 99
REAL ESTATE ECONOMICS AND TECHNOLOGY 100
THE ROAD AHEAD 101
CHAPTER 12: CASE STUDIES IN PROPERTY DEVELOPMENT 102
CASE STUDY 1: THE DEVELOPER'S PERSPECTIVE. PROJECT: RIVERVIEW RESIDENTIAL COMPLEX 103
CASE STUDY 2: THE ENTREPRENEUR'S PERSPECTIVE. PROJECT: CO-WORKING INNOVATION HUB 105
CASE STUDY 3: THE DEALMAKER'S

PERSPECTIVE. PROJECT: URBAN MIXED-USE DEVELOPMENT 107
INTEGRATING LESSONS FROM CASE STUDIES 109
   Key Takeaways: 109
   THE ROAD AHEAD 110
CHAPTER 13: CONCLUSION 111
Updated List of Books to Date 116
Real Estate Mastery Books 117
ACKNOWLEDGEMENTS 118
SOCIAL PROFILES 120
AUTHOR BIO 121
MENTORSHIP, CONSULTING AND PUBLIC SPEAKING 123
Upcoming Projects **125**
We Value Your Feedback! **126**
Portfolio of Books by Willem Tait 127

CHAPTER 1: INTRODUCTION TO PROPERTY DEVELOPMENT

Property development is one of the most dynamic and impactful industries in the world. It's the cornerstone of urban growth, a key driver of economic development, and a powerful tool for wealth creation. But more than anything, it is the art and science of transforming spaces. Whether you're a developer, entrepreneur, or dealmaker, property development represents an unparalleled opportunity to leave your mark on the world, shaping communities and creating long-lasting value.

Imagine standing on a vacant plot of land. What do you see? Some may see emptiness, while others see limitless potential. This is the essence of property development, the ability to envision opportunity where others see nothing. It's a field where visionaries, strategists, and creators come together to transform raw potential into tangible assets, whether it's a residential community, a bustling commercial district, or a state-of-the-art mixed-use complex.

This chapter serves as the foundation for your journey into property development. We'll explore the fundamentals of the industry, its impact on urbanization and infrastructure, and the critical roles played by developers, architects, and investors. By the end, you'll understand why property development is not just about building structures, it's about creating opportunities, solving problems, and leaving a legacy.

THE FOUNDATIONS OF PROPERTY DEVELOPMENT

At its heart, property development is about identifying potential and creating value. It begins with land, the foundation of all real estate endeavors. The process starts with identifying suitable sites, often requiring a deep understanding of market demand, land use regulations, and community needs. Developers must also consider the feasibility of projects, balancing costs, potential revenue, and environmental impact.

For entrepreneurs, property development offers a pathway to innovation and growth. By identifying underutilized spaces or emerging trends, entrepreneurs can create projects that meet modern demands. Dealmakers, on the other hand, focus on structuring agreements and securing financing, ensuring that every project has the resources needed to succeed.

What sets property development apart from other industries is its ability to impact entire communities. A well-planned development can provide housing for families, create jobs, and stimulate economic growth. Conversely, poorly executed projects can lead to environmental degradation, financial loss, and community dissatisfaction. This duality makes property development both a responsibility and an opportunity.

PROPERTY DEVELOPMENT AND URBANIZATION

Urbanization is one of the defining trends of the twenty-first century. As cities expand to accommodate growing populations, the demand for housing, commercial spaces, and public infrastructure is reaching unprecedented levels. Property developers are at the forefront of this transformation, playing a critical role in shaping the future of urban landscapes.

Consider the rapid growth of metropolitan areas worldwide. Cities like New York, London, and Dubai have become global hubs of commerce and culture, largely due to visionary property development. These cities didn't grow organically, they were shaped by strategic planning, investment, and development. Today, developers face new challenges as they work to create sustainable, inclusive, and resilient urban spaces.

Infrastructure is a key component of urban growth. Roads, bridges, utilities, and public services are all necessary to support expanding populations. Property development often acts as a catalyst for these improvements. For example, a new residential community might require expanded transportation networks, while a commercial project could stimulate investment in utilities and public amenities.

For dealmakers, urbanization presents a wealth of opportunities. Structuring partnerships between private developers, public agencies, and investors is critical to ensuring that urban projects are financially viable.

THE ROLE OF DEVELOPERS IN PROPERTY DEVELOPMENT

Developers are the driving force behind every successful project. They are the visionaries who identify opportunities, the strategists who plan projects, and the managers who oversee execution. The role of a developer is multifaceted, requiring a blend of creativity, business acumen, and technical expertise.

A successful developer must wear many hats. They need to understand market dynamics, navigate regulatory environments, and manage construction timelines. They must also build relationships with architects, contractors, and investors, creating a team capable of bringing their vision to life.

One of the most critical skills for developers is risk management. Every project comes with its share of uncertainties, from fluctuating market conditions to unforeseen construction challenges. Developers who can anticipate and mitigate these risks are more likely to succeed in the competitive world of property development.

ARCHITECTS AND THEIR CONTRIBUTION TO DEVELOPMENT

While developers provide the vision, architects bring it to life. They are the creative minds responsible for designing spaces that are functional, aesthetically pleasing, and aligned with the goals of the project. The collaboration between developers and architects is essential to the success of any development. This partnership is a fusion of technical expertise and artistic expression, where the developer's vision is translated into a tangible structure that meets the project's objectives.

Architects play a critical role in balancing practicality and creativity. They must consider the needs of the end users, the constraints of the site, and the goals of the developer. A well-designed project not only enhances property value but also fosters a sense of place, drawing buyers or tenants while contributing positively to the broader community. Architects' ability to innovate within budgetary and regulatory parameters is a testament to their indispensable role in the development process.

For entrepreneurs entering the property development space, understanding the role of architects is crucial. By fostering strong partnerships with design professionals, entrepreneurs can ensure that their projects meet both market demands and aesthetic standards. This collaboration often serves as the foundation for long-term success.

INVESTORS: THE BACKBONE OF PROPERTY DEVELOPMENT

No property development project can succeed without funding. Investors are the backbone of the industry, providing the financial resources needed to turn ideas into reality. From private equity firms to individual backers, investors play a critical role in every stage of the development process.

For dealmakers, working with investors is a key aspect of their role. They must identify potential funding sources, negotiate terms, and ensure that all parties are aligned on the goals of the project. This requires a deep understanding of financial markets, risk assessment, and deal structuring.

Investors are not just passive participants in property development. They often act as strategic partners, providing valuable insights and guidance. For developers and entrepreneurs, building strong relationships with investors is essential to long-term success.

CHALLENGES AND OPPORTUNITIES IN PROPERTY DEVELOPMENT

Every property development project comes with its share of challenges. From navigating complex zoning laws to managing construction delays, developers must be prepared to face a wide range of obstacles. However, these challenges also present opportunities for innovation and growth.

For example, rising construction costs might encourage developers to explore new building materials or techniques. Environmental regulations could lead to the adoption of sustainable practices, creating projects that are both eco-friendly and cost-effective. Market fluctuations might highlight underserved segments, allowing developers to target niche opportunities.

Entrepreneurs and dealmakers thrive in challenging environments. Their ability to adapt, innovate, and negotiate gives them a competitive edge. By approaching challenges with a problem-solving mindset, they can turn obstacles into steppingstones for success.

THE FUTURE OF PROPERTY DEVELOPMENT

The landscape of property development is constantly evolving. Technological advancements, changing demographics, and shifting economic conditions are reshaping the industry. Developers, entrepreneurs, and dealmakers must stay ahead of these trends to remain competitive.

Emerging technologies like artificial intelligence, 3D modeling, and virtual reality are revolutionizing the way projects are planned and executed. Sustainability is becoming a central focus, with developers incorporating green building practices and renewable energy solutions into their projects. These trends are not just shaping the industry, they are defining the future of our cities.

For those new to property development, understanding these trends is crucial.

LAYING THE GROUNDWORK FOR SUCCESS

Property development is more than a career, it's a calling. It's an opportunity to create, innovate, and inspire. Whether you're a developer seeking to refine your skills, an entrepreneur exploring new opportunities, or a dealmaker looking to close your next big deal, this book is your essential guide.

The journey begins here. As you turn the pages, you'll discover the principles, strategies, and insights that drive successful property development. You'll learn how to assess markets, structure deals, manage risks, and execute projects that leave a lasting impact. Each chapter is designed to equip you with practical tools and actionable knowledge, ensuring you're prepared for every step of the process.

This is more than a guide. It's your blueprint for success. With real-world examples and proven techniques, you'll gain the confidence to tackle challenges and seize opportunities. Welcome to the world of property development. Let's get started.

THE ROAD AHEAD

The journey of property development is one of creativity, determination, and strategic thinking. It combines the ability to see potential where others see obstacles, the courage to take calculated risks, and the expertise to execute plans with precision. Whether you are shaping communities, building wealth, or navigating complex deals, the lessons in this book will guide you toward success.

As we conclude this chapter, you now have a foundation for understanding the essence of property development, its opportunities, challenges, and transformative potential. But this is only the beginning. To excel in this field, you must dive deeper into the strategies and tools that turn visions into reality. The next step in your journey starts with understanding your market and identifying the factors that drive successful projects.

Turn the page, and let's explore the critical first stage of every property development project: Market Research and Analysis.

CHAPTER 2: MARKET RESEARCH AND ANALYSIS

Market research is the starting point of every successful property development project. It provides clarity, direction, and actionable insights that allow developers, entrepreneurs, and dealmakers to make informed decisions. Without it, even the most ambitious projects risk failure due to misalignment with market needs and trends.

This chapter focuses on understanding property markets, identifying profitable locations, and assessing demographic needs while anticipating future trends. By mastering market research and analysis, you lay the groundwork for sustainable and profitable development.

UNDERSTANDING THE PROPERTY MARKET

Every property market operates as a living ecosystem, influenced by economic factors, population growth, and local infrastructure. Developers must assess these dynamics to create projects that align with market demand.

The first step in market research is identifying the produce of a market. This means evaluating what the area offers, from its existing developments to its growth potential. For example, an area with high demand for residential housing but limited supply presents a clear opportunity for developers.

Entrepreneurs can capitalize on niche opportunities within the market, while dealmakers rely on this information to structure agreements that maximize value. Understanding market produce is essential for identifying where to invest resources effectively.

IDENTIFYING PROFITABLE LOCATIONS

Location is the foundation of property development success. A well-chosen site can mean the difference between a thriving project and one that struggles to gain traction. Developers must evaluate key factors such as accessibility, proximity to amenities, and the area's growth potential.

Trend analysis plays a vital role here. Identifying neighborhoods poised for expansion allows developers to act ahead of market shifts. For instance, a previously overlooked suburb might become a hotspot due to planned infrastructure improvements like new transportation links or commercial hubs.

Feasibility is equally critical. Developers should analyze zoning laws, environmental concerns, and potential costs. A profitable location must not only align with current market demand but also support long-term growth.

UNDERSTANDING DEMOGRAPHIC NEEDS

The success of a property development project hinges on its ability to meet the needs of the target demographic. Understanding the population of an area, its age groups, income levels, and lifestyle preferences, provides invaluable insights.

For example, an area with many young professionals might demand modern apartments with easy access to work and leisure. In contrast, family-oriented communities may prioritize larger homes with green spaces and schools nearby.

By tailoring projects to fit these needs, developers can produce assets that resonate with buyers and tenants. Entrepreneurs use demographic data to identify underserved markets, while dealmakers structure deals that cater to these demands.

VALUATION AND DEMAND ANALYSIS

Valuation is the process of determining the worth of a property or land based on its features and market position. This assessment is critical for developers to gauge the profitability of a project. Factors like location, infrastructure, and comparable properties influence valuation.

Demand analysis complements valuation by identifying what the market truly needs. Developers must ask questions like: Is there a shortage of affordable housing? Are businesses seeking more office space?

Understanding demand ensures that the produce of the development aligns with market expectations.

By combining valuation and demand analysis, developers can create projects that deliver both financial returns and community value.

TREND FORECASTING AND THE FUTURE OF MARKETS

Property markets are constantly evolving. Developers who anticipate changes in trends are better positioned to succeed in competitive environments. Trend forecasting involves analyzing economic indicators, population growth, and technological advancements to predict future demand.

For example, the rise of remote work has increased demand for suburban properties with home office spaces. Similarly, growing awareness of sustainability has created opportunities for energy-efficient developments.

Feasibility is critical when adapting to these trends. Developers must assess whether their projects can meet future market demands without compromising profitability or practicality.

TOOLS FOR EFFECTIVE MARKET RESEARCH

Modern technology has transformed market research, providing developers with powerful tools to analyze data. Geographic Information Systems (GIS) allow developers to visualize land use and infrastructure. Online tools and platforms offer insights into property values and market trends.

Traditional methods, such as surveys and community outreach, remain valuable for understanding local preferences. Combining quantitative data with qualitative insights gives developers a comprehensive view of the market.

Entrepreneurs and dealmakers can use these tools to identify opportunities, structure deals, and maximize returns. Effective market research is not just about gathering information; it is about using that information to make better decisions.

NAVIGATING MARKET CHALLENGES

Every property market comes with its challenges. Developers must navigate economic shifts, regulatory changes, and unexpected obstacles. These challenges are not just risks, they are opportunities for growth and innovation.

For example, high land costs might lead developers to explore partnerships with local governments or private investors. Changes in demand could prompt a shift in project focus, such as converting planned luxury apartments into more affordable housing.

By staying informed and flexible, developers can turn potential setbacks into steppingstones for success.

THE ROAD AHEAD

Market research and analysis form the backbone of property development. This chapter has outlined the essential steps for understanding markets, assessing opportunities, and anticipating trends.

As you proceed, remember that market research is not a one-time task, it is an ongoing process that evolves with the industry.

In the next chapter, we will explore how to take these insights and apply them to feasibility studies, ensuring that every project is aligned with market realities and financial goals.

CHAPTER 3: FEASIBILITY STUDIES

Feasibility studies are the blueprint of property development. They provide developers, entrepreneurs, and dealmakers with the critical data needed to determine whether a project is viable. This phase of the process moves beyond conceptual ideas into practical evaluations, answering the fundamental question: Will this project succeed?

A comprehensive feasibility study analyzes every aspect of a property project, including costs, market demand, location benefits, and potential return on investment (ROI). By taking a meticulous approach, developers can identify risks, uncover opportunities, and ensure their projects are not only financially sound but also aligned with market needs.

This chapter will guide you through the essential components of feasibility studies, from cost analysis and ROI calculations to site assessments and potential upsides. By mastering these skills, you'll gain the confidence to make informed decisions and minimize uncertainties in every project.

THE PURPOSE OF FEASIBILITY STUDIES

Every property development project begins with a vision, but not every vision is practical. Feasibility studies act as a reality check, evaluating whether a project can move from concept to completion. They provide an in-depth look at the financial, operational, and market factors that influence success.

For developers, a feasibility study ensures that resources are allocated efficiently and that projects are set up for long-term profitability. Entrepreneurs use feasibility studies to secure funding and attract investors, while dealmakers rely on them to negotiate favorable terms.

A well-executed feasibility study answers key questions such as:

- Is the proposed project financially viable?
- Does the market demand the type of development being considered?
- What risks could impact the project, and how can they be mitigated?

By addressing these questions, feasibility studies provide a clear roadmap for moving forward, or a warning to rethink the approach.

COST ANALYSIS: THE FOUNDATION OF FEASIBILITY

Understanding costs is the first step in determining the viability of a property project. Cost analysis involves estimating the total expenses associated with land acquisition, construction, permits, and ongoing maintenance.

Types of Costs to Consider:

1. Land Costs: The price of acquiring the site, including legal fees, surveys, and taxes.
2. Construction Costs: Materials, labor, and contractor fees. These can vary widely

depending on location, design, and market conditions.
3. Soft Costs: Expenses related to design, engineering, and project management.
4. Operational Costs: Long-term expenses such as property management, utilities, and maintenance.

A detailed cost analysis allows developers to create accurate budgets and avoid unexpected expenses. Entrepreneurs can use this data to demonstrate financial responsibility to investors, while dealmakers incorporate it into negotiations to ensure fair agreements.

MARKET DEMAND: ALIGNING PROJECTS WITH NEEDS

A project's success hinges on its ability to meet market demand. Feasibility studies must include a thorough analysis of current and future demand for the type of development being proposed.

Key Factors to Assess:

- Demographics: Who are the potential buyers or tenants? What are their income levels, preferences, and needs?
- Supply and Competition: How many similar properties are available in the area? Is there an oversupply or a gap in the market?
- Future Trends: Are there economic, technological, or social changes that could impact demand?

For example, a feasibility study for a residential project might reveal high demand for affordable housing in the area, but limited interest in luxury apartments. Armed with this information, developers can adjust their plans to align with market realities.

LOCATION BENEFITS: THE IMPORTANCE OF SITE ANALYSIS

Location is one of the most critical factors in property development. A feasibility study must assess the benefits and challenges of the chosen site to determine its suitability for the project.

Components of Site Analysis:

1. Accessibility: Is the site easy to reach via public transport, roads, or pedestrian pathways?
2. Amenities: What facilities and services are nearby, such as schools, hospitals, and shopping centers?
3. Zoning and Regulations: Are there any restrictions on how the site can be developed?
4. Environmental Factors: Does the site have any environmental challenges, such as flood risks or contamination?

A detailed site analysis helps developers identify potential barriers and opportunities. For entrepreneurs, this data is essential for pitching projects to investors, while dealmakers use it to negotiate terms that reflect the site's true value.

RETURN ON INVESTMENT (ROI): MEASURING PROFITABILITY

ROI is the ultimate metric for evaluating a project's success. A feasibility study calculates ROI by comparing the total costs of the project to the expected revenue or value it will generate.

Calculating ROI:

1. Revenue Projections: Estimate the income from sales, rentals, or other revenue streams.
2. Cost Analysis: Factor in all expenses, including construction, marketing, and ongoing operations.
3. Net Profit: Subtract total costs from total revenue to calculate profit.
4. ROI Formula: Divide net profit by total costs, then multiply by 100 to express ROI as a percentage.

For example, if a project costs $1 million and generates $1.5 million in revenue, the ROI is 50 percent. This metric helps developers determine whether a project is worth pursuing and provides a compelling case for investors.

COSTINGS AND BUDGETING: STAYING ON TRACK

Feasibility studies must include detailed costings to ensure projects stay within budget. This involves breaking down expenses into manageable categories and identifying potential cost overruns.

Tips for Effective Costings:

- Use realistic estimates based on current market conditions.
- Include a contingency fund for unexpected expenses.
- Regularly review and update costings as the project progresses.

For dealmakers, costings provide a clear framework for structuring agreements. Entrepreneurs can use costings to demonstrate financial responsibility and build trust with investors.

POTENTIAL UPSIDE: IDENTIFYING OPPORTUNITIES

While feasibility studies focus on risks and challenges, they also highlight potential upsides. These are the opportunities that can maximize a project's value and profitability.

Examples of Potential Upsides:

- Value-Added Features: Adding amenities or design elements that increase appeal and revenue.

- Market Timing: Launching the project at a time when demand is at its peak.
- Partnerships: Collaborating with local governments or businesses to reduce costs and expand reach.

By identifying potential upsides, feasibility studies provide developers with strategies to enhance project outcomes and achieve greater success.

NAVIGATING CHALLENGES THROUGH FEASIBILITY

No project is without risks, and every development effort carries the potential for unexpected challenges. However, a comprehensive feasibility study provides developers with the critical tools and insights needed to anticipate, assess, and address these hurdles effectively.

By carefully analyzing financial, legal, environmental, and market variables, a feasibility study enables developers to make informed decisions that reduce uncertainties and enhance project success. Whether it involves managing escalating costs due to inflation or supply chain disruptions, adapting to shifts in market demand or economic conditions, or addressing site-specific constraints such as zoning restrictions or environmental impacts, a well-executed feasibility study serves as a roadmap.

It not only identifies potential pitfalls early on but also outlines viable strategies to overcome them, ensuring that the project stays aligned with its goals and timeline. This diligence transforms risks into manageable elements of the development process, increasing the likelihood of a successful and profitable outcome.

THE ROAD AHEAD

Feasibility studies are the backbone of property development, providing the data and insights needed to make informed decisions. By mastering cost analysis, market demand, site evaluation, and ROI calculations, developers can minimize risks and maximize rewards.

As you move forward, remember that feasibility is not just about numbers, it's about understanding the bigger picture.

The next chapter will explore how to take the insights gained from feasibility studies and apply them to financial planning and budgeting, ensuring every project is set up for long-term success.

CHAPTER 4: FINANCIAL PLANNING AND BUDGETING

Financial planning and budgeting are the lifeblood of property development. Every successful project, from residential complexes to large-scale commercial ventures, begins with a clear financial strategy. This critical phase determines not only the feasibility of a project but also its long-term profitability. For developers, entrepreneurs, and dealmakers, mastering financial planning is essential to securing funding, controlling costs, and achieving sustainable growth.

The process of financial planning and budgeting involves more than simply balancing numbers. It requires a strategic approach to capital allocation, an understanding of market conditions, and the ability to forecast both risks and opportunities. A strong financial foundation ensures that projects remain viable, even in the face of unexpected challenges.

This chapter provides an in-depth exploration of financial strategies for property development, but readers looking for an even deeper dive into securing funding and building financial success can turn to my other book called *Raising Money for Real Estate Investment: Close Deals, Raise Money, Build Wealth*. Together, these resources will equip you with the tools and insights needed to maximize profitability, minimize risk, and achieve sustainable growth in your real estate ventures.

THE IMPORTANCE OF FINANCIAL STRATEGIES

A well-thought-out financial strategy is the backbone of any property development project. Without it, even the most promising ventures can falter due to cash flow issues, cost overruns, or unforeseen expenses. Financial strategies serve as a roadmap, guiding developers from project inception to completion.

One of the primary goals of financial planning is to align capital with project objectives. Developers must evaluate the costs of land acquisition, construction, marketing, and operations while ensuring sufficient funds are available at each stage. Entrepreneurs use financial strategies to attract investors by demonstrating the potential for high returns, while dealmakers rely on these plans to structure agreements that benefit all parties involved.

Financial strategies are not static; they must be adaptable to changing market conditions and project requirements. A flexible approach allows developers to pivot when necessary, ensuring the project remains on track. By establishing a solid financial plan, developers can navigate complexities with confidence, ultimately maximizing the value of their investments.

PROJECT FUNDING: SOURCES AND STRATEGIES

Securing funding is one of the most significant challenges in property development. Projects often require substantial capital, and developers must explore a variety of funding sources to meet their financial needs. Understanding the options available and their implications is crucial for ensuring a project's success.

Common Sources of Project Funding:

1. Equity Financing: Developers can raise capital by offering equity in the project to investors. This method spreads risk but may require giving up partial ownership.
2. Debt Financing: Loans from banks or financial institutions provide immediate funding but come with the obligation of repayment, often with interest.
3. Private Investors: High-net-worth individuals or venture capitalists may fund projects in exchange for a share of the profits.
4. Government Grants: In some cases, public funding is available for projects that align with community or infrastructure goals.
5. Crowdfunding: An increasingly popular option, crowdfunding allows developers to raise smaller amounts from a large pool of contributors.

Each funding source has its advantages and drawbacks. Equity financing reduces personal risk but dilutes ownership, while debt financing maintains control but increases financial obligations. Entrepreneurs must weigh these factors carefully, selecting the option that best aligns with their goals and risk tolerance.

For dealmakers, project funding is an area of opportunity. Their expertise in structuring deals allows them to secure favorable terms for financing, ensuring that projects remain profitable. By leveraging their network and knowledge, dealmakers play a vital role in connecting developers with the right funding sources.

BUDGETING: CREATING A ROADMAP FOR SUCCESS

A well-crafted budget is more than a financial document, it is a roadmap that outlines how resources will be allocated throughout the project. Budgeting involves identifying all costs associated with the development, estimating revenues, and ensuring that the project remains financially viable.

Key Components of a Development Budget:

- Land Costs: The price of acquiring the site, including associated legal and administrative fees.
- Construction Costs: Materials, labor, and contractor fees. These are often the largest expenses in a project.
- Soft Costs: Design, engineering, permits, and other non-construction-related expenses.
- Marketing Costs: Advertising, staging, and other efforts to attract buyers or tenants.

- Contingency Fund: A reserve for unexpected expenses, typically five to ten percent of the total budget.

Developers must ensure that their budgets are both comprehensive and realistic. Overestimating revenues or underestimating costs can lead to financial difficulties, while an accurate budget provides a clear framework for managing resources.

Budgeting also plays a critical role in risk management. By anticipating potential challenges and allocating funds accordingly, developers can minimize disruptions and keep projects on track. For entrepreneurs, a well-prepared budget is an essential tool for securing investment, while dealmakers use it to negotiate terms that reflect the project's financial realities.

COST CONTROL: MANAGING EXPENSES EFFECTIVELY

Cost control is an integral part of financial planning. Even with a solid budget in place, developers must monitor expenses closely to ensure that costs do not spiral out of control. Effective cost management involves identifying potential areas of overspending, implementing corrective measures, and maintaining financial discipline throughout the project.

Strategies for Cost Control:

1. Regular Monitoring: Conduct frequent reviews of expenses against the budget to identify discrepancies early.

2. Competitive Bidding: Obtain multiple quotes for materials and services to ensure the best value for money.
3. Efficient Resource Allocation: Optimize the use of labor, materials, and equipment to reduce waste.
4. Change Management: Establish a process for evaluating and approving changes to the project scope, ensuring that any adjustments are financially justified.

Cost control is particularly important in large-scale projects, where even minor oversights can lead to significant financial losses. By maintaining a proactive approach, developers can keep expenses within budget and maximize profitability.

For dealmakers, cost control is an area of negotiation. They work to secure favorable pricing and terms from contractors, suppliers, and other stakeholders, ensuring that the project remains financially sustainable.

MAXIMIZING PROFITABILITY

Profitability is the ultimate goal of property development. A successful project not only recovers its costs but also generates significant returns for developers and investors. Financial planning plays a crucial role in maximizing profitability by aligning resources with opportunities.

Factors That Influence Profitability:

- Market Conditions: Timing is critical. Launching a project during periods of high demand can significantly boost returns.
- Value-Added Features: Incorporating amenities or design elements that enhance the project's appeal can justify higher prices.
- Operational Efficiency: Streamlining processes and reducing waste can improve the bottom line.

For entrepreneurs, profitability is a key selling point when attracting investors. By demonstrating the potential for strong returns, they can secure the funding needed to bring their visions to life. Dealmakers, meanwhile, focus on structuring agreements that maximize profits while minimizing risks for all parties involved.

INVESTMENT STRATEGIES: BUILDING LONG-TERM SUCCESS

Investment is not just about funding individual projects; it is about building a sustainable portfolio that generates ongoing returns. Developers must think beyond the immediate project, considering how their financial strategies contribute to long-term growth.

Principles of Investment in Property Development:

- Diversification: Spread investments across multiple projects to reduce risk.
- Reinvestment: Use profits from successful projects to fund new opportunities.

- Market Awareness: Stay informed about economic trends and emerging opportunities.
- Partnerships: Collaborate with investors, governments, and other stakeholders to leverage resources and expertise.

For entrepreneurs, building strong relationships with investors is critical to long-term success. By demonstrating reliability and delivering results, they can establish a reputation that attracts future opportunities. Dealmakers play a pivotal role in facilitating these partnerships, ensuring that all parties benefit from the collaboration.

THE ROAD AHEAD

Financial planning and budgeting are the cornerstones of successful property development. By mastering the principles outlined in this chapter, developers can secure funding, manage costs, and maximize profitability.

These skills not only contribute to individual project success but also lay the foundation for sustainable growth and long-term achievement.

In the next chapter, we will delve into project management, exploring how to coordinate resources, timelines, and stakeholders to bring projects to life efficiently and effectively.

CHAPTER 5: PROJECT MANAGEMENT

Project management is the cornerstone of successful real estate development. It serves as the framework that ensures projects are delivered on time, within budget, and to the satisfaction of all stakeholders. In the fast-paced world of property development, where delays and mismanagement can lead to significant financial losses, mastering project management is not just an asset, it's a necessity.

At its core, project management is about coordination. It involves aligning multiple moving parts, from managing resources and setting timelines to ensuring seamless communication between stakeholders. For developers, entrepreneurs, and dealmakers, understanding and implementing strong project management practices can mean the difference between a project that thrives and one that falters.

This chapter delves into the key elements of project management in real estate development, focusing on scheduling, workflow, resource allocation, stakeholder coordination, and meeting deadlines. By mastering these components, you'll be equipped to lead projects to successful completion while minimizing risks and maximizing returns.

THE ROLE OF PROJECT MANAGEMENT IN REAL ESTATE DEVELOPMENT

Real estate development is a complex process involving numerous stakeholders, including developers, architects, contractors, investors, and regulatory bodies. Each party brings unique expertise to the table, but without a cohesive plan, even the best teams can falter. This is where project management comes in.

Project management provides structure. It establishes a clear roadmap that outlines each phase of the development process, from pre-construction planning to final delivery. By creating a well-defined workflow, project managers ensure that tasks are completed efficiently and that resources are allocated effectively.

For developers, project management is about more than just keeping things on track. It's about anticipating challenges, adapting to changes, and maintaining control over every aspect of the project. Entrepreneurs, on the other hand, use project management to turn visionary ideas into actionable plans, while dealmakers leverage these skills to build trust and collaboration among stakeholders.

In real estate development, project management is not an optional skill, it's an essential one. It ensures that every dollar is spent wisely, every timeline is met, and every stakeholder is satisfied.

SCHEDULING: BUILDING THE FOUNDATION FOR SUCCESS

Scheduling is the backbone of project management. A well-structured schedule serves as a roadmap, outlining when tasks need to be completed and by whom. It provides clarity and direction, ensuring that every team member knows their responsibilities and deadlines.

Key Elements of Effective Scheduling:

- Task Prioritization: Identify critical tasks that must be completed first to avoid delays in subsequent phases.
- Realistic Timelines: Create schedules that account for potential setbacks, such as weather delays or supply chain disruptions.
- Milestones: Break the project into manageable phases, setting clear goals for each stage.
- Flexibility: Build in buffer time to accommodate unexpected changes without derailing the project.

For developers, scheduling ensures that resources are used efficiently and that progress is tracked consistently. Entrepreneurs can use scheduling to streamline workflows and maintain momentum, while dealmakers rely on it to align the expectations of all parties involved.

By creating a comprehensive schedule, you lay the foundation for a project that progresses smoothly and stays on track.

WORKFLOW: STREAMLINING THE DEVELOPMENT PROCESS

Workflow management is about optimizing the sequence of tasks to ensure that resources are used efficiently and that projects move forward without unnecessary delays. In real estate development, where multiple teams often work simultaneously, a well-organized workflow is critical.

Components of Effective Workflow Management:

1. Task Assignment: Clearly define roles and responsibilities for each team member.
2. Process Mapping: Outline the sequence of tasks, ensuring that dependencies are identified and addressed.
3. Communication: Establish regular check-ins and updates to keep all teams aligned.
4. Technology Integration: Use project management tools, such as Trello or Asana, to track progress and facilitate collaboration.

For developers, workflow management minimizes bottlenecks and reduces the risk of errors. Entrepreneurs benefit from streamlined processes that keep projects moving forward, while dealmakers use workflows to ensure that agreements are executed efficiently.

Workflow management is not just about efficiency, it's about creating a system that supports creativity, innovation, and problem-solving.

RESOURCE ALLOCATION: MAXIMIZING EFFICIENCY

Resource allocation is one of the most challenging aspects of project management. Developers must balance competing demands for labor, materials, and financial resources while ensuring that each is used effectively.

Strategies for Effective Resource Allocation:

- Inventory Management: Keep track of materials to avoid shortages or excess stock.
- Labor Scheduling: Assign tasks based on team members' expertise and availability.
- Cost Monitoring: Track expenses to ensure that resources are used within budget.
- Flexibility: Be prepared to reallocate resources as project needs change.

Resource allocation requires a delicate balance. Overcommitting resources to one phase can lead to shortages in another, while underutilization can result in wasted time and money. Developers who excel in resource allocation can optimize efficiency and maintain control over project costs.

For entrepreneurs, effective resource management is a key selling point for attracting investors. Dealmakers, meanwhile, use resource allocation strategies to negotiate terms that maximize value for all stakeholders.

COORDINATION: BRINGING STAKEHOLDERS TOGETHER

Real estate development is a team effort. Successful projects require the collaboration of multiple stakeholders, each with their own priorities and expectations. Coordination is the glue that holds these teams together, ensuring that everyone works toward a common goal.

Best Practices for Stakeholder Coordination:

- Regular Updates: Schedule meetings and progress reports to keep everyone informed.
- Clear Communication: Use concise language to convey goals, expectations, and updates.
- Conflict Resolution: Address disagreements quickly to prevent them from escalating.
- Shared Vision: Align all stakeholders on the project's objectives and outcomes.

For developers, coordination is about fostering trust and transparency. Entrepreneurs use coordination to maintain momentum and ensure that everyone is on the same page, while dealmakers facilitate collaboration through effective communication and negotiation.

Coordination is not just about managing relationships, it's about building a culture of teamwork and shared success.

MEETING DEADLINES: DELIVERING ON TIME

In real estate development, time is money. Delays can lead to increased costs, strained relationships, and missed opportunities. Meeting deadlines is a critical aspect of project management, requiring careful planning and execution.

Strategies for Meeting Deadlines:

1. Set Realistic Goals: Avoid overpromising by creating achievable timelines.
2. Monitor Progress: Regularly assess the status of tasks to identify potential delays.
3. Address Issues Early: Resolve challenges as soon as they arise to prevent them from compounding.
4. Celebrate Milestones: Recognize achievements to maintain team morale and momentum.

For developers, meeting deadlines demonstrates reliability and competence. Entrepreneurs can use timely project delivery to build their reputation and attract future opportunities, while dealmakers use it to strengthen partnerships and secure long-term relationships.

Delivering on time is not just about staying on schedule, it's about exceeding expectations and setting the stage for future success.

THE ROAD AHEAD

Project management is the engine that drives real estate development. By mastering the principles of scheduling, workflow, resource allocation, coordination, and meeting deadlines, developers can ensure that projects are completed efficiently and profitably.

This chapter has provided a comprehensive guide to project management, equipping you with the tools and strategies needed to lead successful developments. As you move forward, remember that project management is not just a skill, it's a mindset. Approach each project with clarity, adaptability, and a commitment to excellence, and you'll be well on your way to achieving your goals.

In the next chapter, we will explore the legal and regulatory considerations that shape real estate development, providing insights into compliance, risk management, and navigating complex frameworks.

CHAPTER 6: LEGAL AND REGULATORY CONSIDERATIONS

Legal and regulatory considerations are the foundation of every successful property development project. From zoning laws and building codes to contracts and compliance, navigating the legal landscape is essential for avoiding delays, penalties, and costly disputes. Developers, entrepreneurs, and dealmakers who understand these frameworks are better equipped to manage risks and capitalize on opportunities.

In property development, the legal environment serves as both a guide and a safeguard. It establishes the rules that govern how land can be used, how buildings must be constructed, and how stakeholders interact throughout the development process. Compliance with these rules is not optional, it's a critical factor in ensuring the smooth execution of projects.

This chapter explores the key legal and regulatory considerations in property development, focusing on zoning laws, building codes, permits, contracts, and compliance. It also highlights insights from my book, *Real Estate Law Essentials: Navigate Contracts to Avoid Pitfalls and Seize Opportunities*. Readers seeking a deeper dive into the legal aspects of real estate are encouraged to explore that resource for a comprehensive understanding.

COMPLIANCE: THE CORNERSTONE OF SUCCESS

Compliance is the backbone of legal and regulatory considerations. It ensures that projects adhere to the laws and regulations governing property development, reducing the risk of disputes, penalties, or project shutdowns. Developers who prioritize compliance build trust with stakeholders and establish a strong foundation for success.

Key Areas of Compliance in Property Development:

- **Zoning Laws:** Define how land can be used, whether for residential, commercial, industrial, or mixed purposes.
- **Building Codes:** Establish safety and quality standards for construction, covering everything from structural integrity to fire safety.
- **Environmental Regulations:** Govern the impact of development on the natural environment, including waste management and resource conservation.

For developers, compliance is not just a legal requirement, it's a competitive advantage. By demonstrating a commitment to following regulations, developers can secure permits more efficiently, attract investors, and foster positive relationships with local authorities. Entrepreneurs can leverage compliance as a selling point to build credibility, while dealmakers use it to negotiate terms that align with legal frameworks.

ZONING: DEFINING LAND USE

Zoning laws are one of the most critical regulatory frameworks in property development. They dictate how land can be used, specifying permissible activities, building types, and density levels within a given area. Understanding and navigating zoning regulations is essential for determining the feasibility of a project.

Common Zoning Classifications:

- **Residential Zoning:** Governs single-family homes, apartments, and other living spaces.
- **Commercial Zoning:** Covers office buildings, retail spaces, and other business establishments.
- **Industrial Zoning:** Applies to factories, warehouses, and other facilities involved in manufacturing or distribution.
- **Mixed-Use Zoning:** Allows for a combination of residential, commercial, and sometimes industrial uses within a single development.

Developers must ensure that their projects align with zoning requirements to avoid costly delays or legal challenges. In some cases, zoning laws may require modifications or variances. Entrepreneurs exploring innovative projects, such as co-living spaces or eco-friendly developments, may find opportunities in areas with flexible or evolving zoning laws. Dealmakers play a crucial role in navigating zoning complexities, securing approvals, and structuring agreements that comply with these regulations.

BUILDING CODES: ENSURING SAFETY AND QUALITY

Building codes are another essential component of property development. They establish standards for construction, ensuring that buildings are safe, durable, and fit for their intended use. Compliance with building codes is not just a legal obligation, it's a moral responsibility to protect the safety and well-being of occupants and the surrounding community.

Key Aspects of Building Codes:

- **Structural Standards:** Include requirements for load-bearing walls, foundations, and roofs to ensure stability.
- **Fire Safety:** Cover fire exits, sprinkler systems, and materials used to minimize fire risks.
- **Accessibility:** Mandate features such as ramps, elevators, and other accommodations for individuals with disabilities.
- **Energy Efficiency:** Promote sustainable construction practices, including insulation, lighting, and renewable energy systems.

For developers, understanding building codes is critical for avoiding construction delays and costly rework. Entrepreneurs can use compliance with building codes as a marketing advantage, highlighting safety and quality as selling points. Dealmakers facilitate collaboration between architects, contractors, and regulatory bodies to ensure that all parties meet these standards.

PERMITS: NAVIGATING THE APPROVAL PROCESS

Permits are the formal approvals required to proceed with various stages of property development. They serve as evidence that a project complies with zoning laws, building codes, and other regulations. Obtaining permits is a complex process: Common Types of Permits in Property Development:

- **Land Use Permits:** Approve the intended use of a site based on zoning regulations.
- **Building Permits:** Authorize construction activities, ensuring compliance with building codes.
- **Environmental Permits:** Address the impact of development on the environment, such as water usage and waste disposal.
- **Occupancy Permits:** Certify that a building is safe and ready for use upon completion.

The permit process can be time-consuming, but it is a necessary step in ensuring that projects adhere to legal standards. Developers who approach permitting proactively, by preparing comprehensive applications and maintaining open communication with authorities, can minimize delays and avoid penalties.

For entrepreneurs, navigating the permit process demonstrates professionalism and diligence, qualities that attract investors and build trust. Dealmakers play a pivotal role in securing permits, leveraging their expertise to streamline the approval process and negotiate favorable terms.

CONTRACTS: BUILDING TRUST AND CLARITY

Contracts are the legal agreements that define the roles, responsibilities, and expectations of all parties involved in a property development project. They serve as the foundation for collaboration, ensuring that everyone works toward the same goals while minimizing the risk of disputes.

Key Elements of Effective Contracts:

- **Scope of Work:** Clearly outlines the tasks and deliverables expected from each party.
- **Payment Terms:** Specifies how and when payments will be made, including contingencies for delays or changes.
- **Timelines:** Establishes deadlines for milestones, ensuring accountability.
- **Dispute Resolution:** Includes provisions for addressing conflicts, such as mediation or arbitration clauses.

My book, *Real Estate Law Essentials: Navigate Contracts to Avoid Pitfalls and Seize Opportunities*, provides a comprehensive guide to understanding and drafting contracts in the context of property development. Readers who want to deepen their knowledge of contract law and its application to real estate are encouraged to explore this resource. As the author, I have distilled years of experience into actionable insights that help developers, entrepreneurs, and dealmakers navigate complex legal landscapes with confidence.

RISK MANAGEMENT THROUGH LEGAL COMPLIANCE

Legal and regulatory considerations are not just about meeting requirements, they are about managing risk. By adhering to zoning laws, building codes, and contractual obligations, developers can minimize the likelihood of disputes, fines, or project delays.

Strategies for Risk Management:

- Conduct regular compliance audits to ensure adherence to regulations.
- Build relationships with legal experts and consultants who specialize in property development.
- Stay informed about changes in laws and regulations that could impact your project.

For developers, risk management through compliance is a proactive approach that protects both their investments and their reputation. Entrepreneurs use these strategies to build trust with stakeholders, while dealmakers incorporate risk mitigation into their negotiations.

THE ROAD AHEAD

Legal and regulatory considerations are a fundamental aspect of property development. By understanding zoning laws, building codes, permits, contracts, and compliance, developers can navigate complex legal frameworks with confidence and efficiency.

This chapter has provided an overview of the key legal considerations in property development, but readers seeking a deeper understanding are encouraged to explore my book, *Real Estate Law Essentials: Navigate Contracts to Avoid Pitfalls and Seize Opportunities*. Together, these resources will equip you with the knowledge and tools to succeed in even the most challenging regulatory environments.

In the next chapter, we will examine the construction and development process, focusing on how to transform visions into reality through effective planning, execution, and quality assurance.

CHAPTER 7: CONSTRUCTION AND DEVELOPMENT PROCESS

The construction and development process is where vision meets reality. It is the stage in property development where ideas are transformed into tangible structures, from site preparation to final inspection. This phase requires precision, coordination, and unwavering attention to detail, as every decision made during construction has long-lasting implications for the success and profitability of the project.

For developers, the construction and development process is a journey of execution, where plans are brought to life through meticulous management of resources, materials, and labor. Entrepreneurs approach this phase as an opportunity to innovate, ensuring that the final product meets market demand and stands out in a competitive landscape. Dealmakers view construction as a critical period for maintaining relationships with stakeholders and ensuring that all agreements are fulfilled.

This chapter outlines the steps involved in the construction and development process, offering insights into best practices for property developers, entrepreneurs, and dealmakers. By understanding each stage and its challenges, you will be better equipped to guide your projects from concept to completion.

SITE PREPARATION: LAYING THE GROUNDWORK

Site preparation is the first step in the construction and development process. It involves preparing the land for building, addressing any physical or regulatory challenges that may impact the project. This stage sets the tone for the entire development, as a poorly prepared site can lead to costly delays and complications.

Key Steps in Site Preparation:

- **Land Clearing:** Removing vegetation, debris, and existing structures to create a clean slate for construction.
- **Soil Testing:** Evaluating the soil's stability and suitability for the intended structure.
- **Site Grading:** Leveling the land to ensure proper drainage and foundation stability.
- **Utility Connections:** Establishing access to essential services such as water, electricity, and sewage.

For developers, site preparation is about efficiency and foresight. They must anticipate potential challenges, such as environmental concerns or zoning restrictions, and address them proactively. Entrepreneurs use site preparation as an opportunity to optimize the layout of the project, ensuring that the design maximizes the site's potential. Dealmakers focus on securing the necessary permits and approvals, ensuring that the project can proceed without legal or regulatory hurdles.

DESIGN AND PLANNING: TURNING IDEAS INTO BLUEPRINTS

The design phase is where creativity and functionality intersect. It involves translating the project's vision into detailed plans and blueprints that guide the construction process. This stage requires close collaboration between developers, architects, and engineers to ensure that the design aligns with market demand, budget constraints, and regulatory requirements.

Key Elements of the Design Phase:

- **Conceptual Design:** Developing initial sketches and layouts that capture the project's vision.
- **Architectural Design:** Creating detailed plans that define the structure's dimensions, materials, and aesthetics.
- **Engineering Design:** Addressing structural integrity, utilities, and environmental factors.
- **Permitting:** Submitting designs for approval by local authorities to ensure compliance with building codes and regulations.

Developers approach design with a focus on practicality and feasibility, ensuring that the plans can be executed within the project's budget and timeline. Entrepreneurs prioritize marketability, incorporating features and amenities that enhance the project's appeal. Dealmakers play a critical role in aligning all stakeholders on the design's goals and securing agreements that support the project's vision.

MATERIALS AND SUPPLY CHAIN: BUILDING BLOCKS OF SUCCESS

Materials are the backbone of construction, and their selection and management can significantly impact a project's quality, cost, and timeline. The supply chain for construction materials involves sourcing, procurement, and logistics, all of which must be carefully coordinated to ensure that the project stays on schedule and within budget.

Key Considerations for Material Management:

- **Quality:** Selecting materials that meet safety and durability standards.
- **Cost:** Balancing quality with affordability to optimize the project's budget.
- **Sustainability:** Choosing eco-friendly materials that align with modern market demands.
- **Logistics:** Coordinating the timely delivery of materials to avoid delays.

For developers, material management is about ensuring that the project's foundation is strong and reliable. Entrepreneurs see this stage as an opportunity to differentiate their projects by incorporating innovative or sustainable materials. Dealmakers focus on negotiating favorable terms with suppliers and contractors, ensuring that resources are used efficiently and effectively.

CONSTRUCTION MANAGEMENT: BRINGING THE PROJECT TO LIFE

Construction management is the heart of the development process. It involves overseeing the execution of the project, ensuring that each phase is completed according to plan. This stage requires coordination among contractors, laborers, and supervisors, as well as constant monitoring of progress and quality.

Key Components of Construction Management:

- **Project Scheduling:** Creating and maintaining timelines for each phase of construction.
- **Resource Allocation:** Ensuring that labor, equipment, and materials are used efficiently.
- **Quality Control:** Conducting inspections to ensure that the work meets design specifications and safety standards.
- **Problem Solving:** Addressing unexpected challenges, such as weather delays or supply chain disruptions.

For developers, construction management is about maintaining control over every aspect of the project. Entrepreneurs use this stage to refine their vision, ensuring that the final product meets market expectations. Dealmakers focus on maintaining relationships with contractors and stakeholders, ensuring that all agreements are honored and that the project stays on track.

INSPECTION AND QUALITY ASSURANCE: DELIVERING EXCELLENCE

The final stages of the construction process involve inspection and quality assurance, where the completed structure is evaluated to ensure that it meets all legal, regulatory, and contractual requirements. This stage is critical for obtaining occupancy permits and delivering a product that satisfies stakeholders.

Key Steps in Inspection and Quality Assurance:

- **Final Inspections:** Verifying that the building complies with safety and building codes.
- **Punch Lists:** Addressing any minor issues or defects identified during inspections.
- **Occupancy Certification:** Securing permits that authorize the building's use.
- **Handover:** Delivering the completed project to stakeholders, including buyers, tenants, or investors.

For developers, this stage represents the culmination of their efforts and the realization of their vision. Entrepreneurs use the handover as an opportunity to showcase the project's value, while dealmakers ensure that all contractual obligations are fulfilled and that stakeholders are satisfied with the final result.

THE PERSPECTIVES OF DEVELOPERS, ENTREPRENEURS, AND DEALMAKERS

The construction and development process is multifaceted, with each stakeholder bringing a unique perspective to the table. Developers focus on execution, balancing budgets and timelines while ensuring that the project meets design and quality standards. Entrepreneurs approach construction as an opportunity to innovate, incorporating features and materials that enhance marketability. Dealmakers see the process as a collaborative effort, ensuring that all parties work together harmoniously to achieve the project's goals.

By understanding these perspectives, you can navigate the complexities of construction with confidence and clarity. Each stakeholder plays a vital role in bringing the project to life, and their collaboration is the key to success.

THE ROAD AHEAD

The construction and development process is the heart of property development. By mastering the steps outlined in this chapter, site preparation, design and planning, materials management, construction, and quality assurance, you can transform concepts into completed properties that stand the test of time.

This chapter has provided a comprehensive guide to the construction process, offering insights into the roles and responsibilities of developers, entrepreneurs, and dealmakers.

In the next chapter, we will explore marketing and sales strategies, focusing on how to position completed projects for success in the marketplace.

CHAPTER 8: MARKETING AND SALES STRATEGIES

Marketing and sales strategies are the engines that drive the success of property development projects. These strategies connect a development's vision with the needs of buyers and tenants, turning completed units into thriving spaces. For developers, entrepreneurs, and dealmakers, the ability to position properties effectively and execute tailored sales techniques is essential for maximizing returns and ensuring the long-term viability of a project.

This chapter explores how to position properties in the market, create compelling branding, and implement targeted sales strategies. It also provides a deep dive into pre-selling and pre-letting techniques, which are critical for securing early commitments and reducing financial risks. Whether your project is residential or commercial, these insights will help you navigate the marketing and sales process with clarity and confidence.

For a more comprehensive understanding of these concepts, refer to my books *Practical Principles of Commercial Real Estate Investment, Tasks and Strategies for Real Estate Success* and *Proven Principles of Residential Real Estate Investment, Strategies and Tasks for Building Generational Wealth*. Both books offer detailed strategies tailored to the unique challenges of commercial and residential property development.

POSITIONING PROPERTIES: BUILDING A BRAND

Property positioning is the foundation of effective marketing and sales. It involves creating a clear and compelling identity for a development, one that resonates with the target audience and highlights the project's unique value propositions. Successful positioning ensures that buyers and tenants see the property as the solution to their needs.

Key Steps in Property Positioning:

1. **Identify the Target Market:** Understand who your ideal buyers or tenants are. Are you targeting young professionals, families, or businesses?
2. **Highlight Unique Features:** Showcase the aspects that set your project apart, such as location, design, or amenities.
3. **Create a Brand Identity:** Develop a cohesive visual and verbal identity that communicates the project's values and appeal.
4. **Align with Market Trends:** Incorporate features and benefits that reflect current demand, such as sustainability or tech-enabled spaces.

For developers, positioning is about aligning the project's identity with market demand. Entrepreneurs approach positioning as an opportunity to create a distinct brand that stands out in a crowded market. Dealmakers focus on crafting narratives that appeal to investors, buyers, and tenants alike, ensuring that all stakeholders see the value in the development.

PRE-SELLING AND PRE-LETTING: CREATING EARLY MOMENTUM

Pre-selling and pre-letting are essential strategies for mitigating risk and generating early momentum in property development. These approaches involve securing commitments from buyers or tenants before construction is completed, providing financial stability and reducing the time to profitability.

Benefits of Pre-Selling and Pre-Letting:

- **Financial Security:** Early sales or leases provide cash flow to fund construction and operations.
- **Market Validation:** Demonstrates demand for the project, attracting additional buyers or tenants.
- **Reduced Risk:** Minimizes the financial burden of holding unsold or unleased units.

Strategies for Pre-Selling and Pre-Letting:

1. **Launch Exclusive Promotions:** Offer limited-time incentives, such as discounted pricing or upgraded features, to encourage early commitments.
2. **Host Preview Events:** Invite prospective buyers or tenants to exclusive tours of the site or show units.
3. **Leverage Digital Marketing:** Use social media, email campaigns, and targeted ads to generate interest and drive inquiries.

4. **Collaborate with Agents:** Partner with real estate agents who specialize in the local market to reach a wider audience.

Developers see pre-selling and pre-letting as critical for managing cash flow and reducing risk. Entrepreneurs use these strategies to build excitement and establish a strong market presence. Dealmakers play a pivotal role in negotiating terms and closing agreements that secure early commitments.

MARKETING DURING CONSTRUCTION: MAINTAINING INTEREST

Marketing doesn't stop once pre-sales or pre-leases are secured. During construction, maintaining interest and engagement is essential for attracting additional buyers or tenants and keeping stakeholders informed about the project's progress.

Best Practices for Marketing During Construction:

- **Progress Updates:** Share regular updates, including photos, videos, and milestones, to showcase progress and build anticipation.
- **Community Engagement:** Host events or provide updates that involve the local community, fostering goodwill and awareness.
- **Feature Stories:** Highlight the people, processes, or unique aspects of the project in marketing materials to create an emotional connection.

- **Adapt Campaigns:** Adjust marketing messages based on market feedback or changing conditions.

For developers, mid-construction marketing is about maintaining momentum and addressing any concerns that arise. Entrepreneurs use this stage to refine their messaging and strengthen their brand, while dealmakers ensure that stakeholder relationships remain strong and collaborative.

POST-COMPLETION MARKETING: MAXIMIZING VALUE

Once the project is complete, the focus shifts to selling or leasing the remaining units and maximizing the property's value. Post-completion marketing is about leveraging the development's finished state to attract buyers or tenants who may have been hesitant during earlier phases.

Post-Completion Strategies:

- **Grand Openings:** Host events that showcase the completed property and its features.
- **Testimonials:** Share feedback from early buyers or tenants to build trust and credibility.
- **Enhanced Campaigns:** Use professional photography, virtual tours, and updated branding to highlight the property's finished state.
- **On-Site Agents:** Employ dedicated sales or leasing agents to provide personalized tours and close deals.

Developers see post-completion marketing as the final step in realizing the project's financial potential. Entrepreneurs focus on creating a lasting impression that strengthens their brand, while dealmakers use this phase to solidify relationships and explore future opportunities.

SALES STRATEGIES: CLOSING THE DEAL

Sales strategies are the culmination of the marketing process. They involve converting interest into commitments, whether through purchase agreements or lease contracts. Effective sales techniques require a deep understanding of the target audience, a strong value proposition, and excellent communication skills.

Key Sales Techniques:

- **Build Relationships:** Establish trust and rapport with buyers or tenants to foster long-term relationships.
- **Overcome Objections:** Address concerns or hesitations with clear, fact-based responses.
- **Create Urgency:** Use limited-time offers or scarcity tactics to encourage immediate action.
- **Leverage Data:** Use market insights and project-specific data to demonstrate value.

Developers see sales as the final step in achieving their financial goals. Entrepreneurs use this phase to solidify their reputation and generate referrals, while dealmakers focus on ensuring that all agreements are legally sound and mutually beneficial.

INSIGHTS FROM MY BOOKS

For those seeking a deeper understanding of marketing and sales in property development, my books *Practical Principles of Commercial Real Estate Investment, Tasks and Strategies for Real Estate Success* and *Proven Principles of Residential Real Estate Investment, Strategies and Tasks for Building Generational Wealth* provide detailed guidance.

These resources offer actionable strategies tailored to both commercial and residential projects, helping you navigate the complexities of marketing and sales with confidence.

Whether you're positioning a commercial property for corporate tenants or branding a residential development for families, these books provide the tools and insights needed to succeed. Readers can use these principles to enhance their understanding of marketing and sales, regardless of the project's scale or scope.

THE ROAD AHEAD

Marketing and sales strategies are critical for turning property developments into financial successes. By mastering the principles of property positioning, pre-selling, pre-letting, and targeted sales techniques, you can ensure that your projects attract the right buyers and tenants, maximizing value at every stage.

This chapter has provided a comprehensive overview of the marketing and sales process, offering insights into the perspectives of developers, entrepreneurs, and dealmakers.

In the next chapter, we will explore risk management strategies, focusing on how to identify, assess, and mitigate risks to ensure the long-term success of your developments.

CHAPTER 9: RISK MANAGEMENT

Risk management is the most crucial chapter in this book because it ties together every aspect of property development, entrepreneurship, and dealmaking. Without a firm grasp of risk and how to mitigate it, even the best-laid plans can falter. However, understanding risk is not about avoiding it, it's about identifying, planning for, and navigating through it to achieve success.

Property development, dealmaking, and entrepreneurship are inherently risky endeavors. Market volatility can shift demand overnight, construction delays can derail timelines and budgets, and financial setbacks can destabilize a project or business. Each of these risks must be anticipated, managed, and mitigated to protect investments and capitalize on opportunities.

This chapter explores how risks manifest in the roles of developers, entrepreneurs, and dealmakers. We will delve into strategies to spot and assess risks, implement contingency plans, and turn uncertainty into an advantage.

UNDERSTANDING RISK: A FOUNDATION FOR SUCCESS

Risk is uncertainty, it is the possibility of an outcome differing from what was expected. In property development, this uncertainty can stem from fluctuating market conditions, unexpected construction issues, or unforeseen financial obstacles. For entrepreneurs and dealmakers, risks also include reputational damage, strained partnerships, and failed negotiations.

Types of Risks in Real Estate:

1. **Market Volatility:** Changes in supply and demand, interest rates, or economic conditions.
2. **Construction Delays:** Weather conditions, labor shortages, or material price fluctuations.
3. **Financial Setbacks:** Unsecured funding, cost overruns, or mismanagement of cash flow.
4. **Regulatory Risks:** Changes in zoning laws, building codes, or environmental regulations.

Effective risk management involves more than just reacting to challenges. It requires proactively identifying risks, assessing their potential impact, and planning strategies to address them before they materialize.

THE PROPERTY DEVELOPER'S PERSPECTIVE

For property developers, risk management begins with the initial planning stages and continues through to project completion. Developers must balance budgets, timelines, and stakeholder expectations while navigating external uncertainties like market demand and regulatory requirements.

Key Risks for Developers:

- **Market Volatility:** Developers rely on market research to predict demand, but unexpected economic shifts can render even the most promising projects unprofitable.

- **Construction Delays:** Delays in acquiring permits, supply chain disruptions, or contractor disputes can significantly impact timelines and budgets.
- **Budget Overruns:** Unanticipated costs can erode profit margins, especially if contingency funds are insufficient.

Mitigation Strategies for Developers:

1. **Thorough Market Research:** As outlined in Chapter 2, comprehensive market analysis helps developers anticipate demand and adjust projects accordingly.
2. **Contingency Planning:** Allocate 10–15% of the total budget as a buffer for unexpected expenses.
3. **Contractual Safeguards:** Ensure contracts with contractors and suppliers include clauses for delays and penalties to protect timelines and costs.
4. **Regular Monitoring:** Use project management tools to track progress and address issues early, as discussed in Chapter 5.

For developers, successful risk management means staying adaptable, maintaining open communication with stakeholders, and always preparing for the unexpected.

THE ENTREPRENEUR'S PERSPECTIVE

Entrepreneurs in real estate often face risks tied to innovation and market differentiation. Their ability to take calculated risks is what sets them apart, but this same quality requires them to be vigilant and prepared.

Key Risks for Entrepreneurs:

- **Market Misalignment:** A product or service that doesn't resonate with the target audience can lead to lost revenue.
- **Overextension:** Scaling too quickly or taking on multiple projects without sufficient resources can lead to burnout or financial strain.
- **Funding Challenges:** Securing capital for innovative projects can be difficult, especially in volatile markets.

Mitigation Strategies for Entrepreneurs:

1. **Market Validation:** Test ideas with small pilot projects to assess feasibility before scaling.
2. **Diversified Revenue Streams:** Reduce dependency on a single project or market by diversifying income sources.
3. **Strong Investor Relations:** Build trust with investors through transparent communication and consistent results, as discussed in Chapters 3 and 4.
4. **Scenario Planning:** Develop multiple scenarios for market conditions and plan responses for each.

Entrepreneurs must embrace uncertainty as part of their journey but should always anchor their decisions in data, strategy, and a willingness to pivot when necessary.

THE DEALMAKER'S PERSPECTIVE

Dealmakers operate in a world of negotiations and partnerships, where risks often stem from people rather than projects. Managing these risks requires exceptional interpersonal skills and a deep understanding of legal and financial frameworks.

Key Risks for Dealmakers:

- **Failed Negotiations:** Inability to reach agreements can stall or derail projects.
- **Reputational Damage:** A single misstep in handling partnerships or agreements can tarnish credibility.
- **Contractual Risks:** Poorly structured agreements can lead to disputes or financial losses.

Mitigation Strategies for Dealmakers:

1. **Comprehensive Due Diligence:** Verify the financial and operational viability of partners and projects before committing.
2. **Legal Expertise:** Work closely with legal teams to draft airtight contracts, as highlighted in Chapter 6.
3. **Relationship Building:** Invest time in nurturing partnerships to build trust and mutual respect.

4. **Exit Strategies:** Always have a plan for withdrawing from agreements without jeopardizing other interests.

For dealmakers, risk management is about balancing assertiveness with diplomacy, ensuring that every deal benefits all parties while minimizing potential fallout.

CAPITAL MARKETS AND RISK MANAGEMENT

Understanding capital markets is essential for mastering risk management. The flow of money and investment shapes property markets, influencing everything from interest rates to the availability of financing. My book, *Capital, Markets, and Real Estate: How Money and Capital Shapes the Property Market*, delves into these dynamics, offering insights into how capital markets impact real estate and the risks associated with them.

Readers who seek a deeper understanding of risk management in real estate should explore this book. It provides actionable strategies for navigating market uncertainties, securing funding, and mitigating financial risks.

By understanding the interplay between capital markets and property development, you gain a broader perspective on risk and the tools to manage it effectively.

STRATEGIES FOR EFFECTIVE RISK MANAGEMENT

Risk management is not a one-size-fits-all solution, it requires a tailored approach based on the specific challenges and opportunities of each project. However, some universal strategies can help developers, entrepreneurs, and dealmakers navigate uncertainty.

Universal Risk Management Strategies:

- **Comprehensive Planning:** Develop detailed plans that address every stage of the project, from inception to completion.
- **Proactive Communication:** Maintain open lines of communication with stakeholders to address concerns early.
- **Diversification:** Spread investments across multiple projects or markets to reduce exposure to individual risks.
- **Continuous Learning:** Stay informed about market trends, regulatory changes, and emerging risks.

Effective risk management is not about eliminating uncertainty, it's about building resilience and adaptability. By anticipating challenges and planning for contingencies, you can turn risks into opportunities.

THE ROAD AHEAD

Risk management is the most important aspect of property development, entrepreneurship, and dealmaking. It ties together all the insights from this book, providing a framework for navigating uncertainty and achieving success.

By understanding risks, planning for contingencies, and implementing mitigation strategies, you can protect your investments and position yourself for long-term growth.

This chapter has provided a comprehensive overview of risk management, from identifying potential challenges to implementing actionable solutions.

As you move forward in your journey, remember that every risk carries the potential for reward, if you have the tools to manage it effectively.

CHAPTER 10: SUSTAINABILITY AND GREEN DEVELOPMENT

Sustainability and green development are no longer optional in the world of property development, they are essential. With increasing awareness of environmental challenges, consumers, investors, and governments are demanding eco-friendly practices that prioritize energy efficiency, resource conservation, and reduced environmental impact. For developers, entrepreneurs, and dealmakers, embracing sustainability is not just about meeting these demands; it's about seizing opportunities to innovate, save costs, and build a reputation for responsibility and forward-thinking.

This chapter explores the growing importance of sustainability and green development in property markets. It examines how sustainable practices can be integrated into construction techniques, deal structuring, and entrepreneurship to drive value for all stakeholders. Far from being a burden or obstacle, sustainability offers a competitive edge that can enhance branding, attract investments, and secure financing.

Sustainability is not just a trend, it's a framework for the future of real estate. For those looking to deepen their understanding, my book *Real Estate Economics, Property, Markets, Principles, and Practices* offers detailed insights into the economic principles underpinning sustainability in real estate. By mastering these principles, developers and dealmakers can position themselves as leaders in an evolving market.

THE SHIFT TOWARD SUSTAINABILITY IN REAL ESTATE

The real estate industry is at the forefront of the sustainability movement, driven by both regulatory pressures and market demand. Developers, entrepreneurs, and dealmakers must understand the motivations behind this shift to fully capitalize on its opportunities.

Key Drivers of Sustainability:

1. **Consumer Demand:** Buyers and tenants increasingly prefer properties that are energy-efficient and environmentally friendly.
2. **Regulatory Compliance:** Governments are implementing stricter environmental standards, such as energy codes and emissions regulations.
3. **Investor Preferences:** Investors prioritize projects with sustainable practices, viewing them as lower-risk and future-proof.
4. **Cost Savings:** Sustainable buildings often have lower operational costs due to energy and water efficiency.

For developers, sustainability is an opportunity to align their projects with these drivers. Entrepreneurs can leverage green development as a unique selling point, while dealmakers use sustainability to attract investors and secure favorable terms.

GREEN BUILDING AND ECO-FRIENDLY CONSTRUCTION

Green building practices focus on reducing the environmental impact of construction and creating properties that are efficient, healthy, and adaptable. Developers who embrace these techniques can not only meet regulatory requirements but also appeal to eco-conscious consumers and investors.

Key Features of Green Buildings:

- **Energy Efficiency:** Incorporating solar panels, energy-efficient HVAC systems, and LED lighting.
- **Water Conservation:** Installing low-flow fixtures, rainwater harvesting systems, and efficient irrigation.
- **Sustainable Materials:** Using recycled, renewable, or locally sourced materials.
- **Indoor Air Quality:** Ensuring proper ventilation and using non-toxic materials to promote occupant health.

Developers who prioritize green building practices often find that these features enhance the value and marketability of their properties. For entrepreneurs, green development provides an avenue to innovate and differentiate their offerings. Dealmakers play a critical role in structuring agreements that incorporate sustainability measures, ensuring that all stakeholders benefit.

THE BUSINESS CASE FOR SUSTAINABILITY

Sustainability is often perceived as an added cost, but in reality, it offers significant financial and branding benefits. For developers, entrepreneurs, and dealmakers, understanding these benefits is key to leveraging sustainability as an advantage rather than a burden.

Benefits of Sustainability:

- **Cost Savings:** Energy-efficient buildings reduce utility bills, while sustainable construction practices minimize waste.
- **Enhanced Marketability:** Eco-friendly properties attract buyers and tenants who are willing to pay a premium for sustainability.
- **Risk Mitigation:** Compliance with environmental regulations reduces the risk of fines or project delays.
- **Access to Capital:** Many investors and lenders offer incentives or favorable terms for green projects.

For developers, the ability to present sustainability as a value-adding feature strengthens their position in negotiations. Entrepreneurs can use sustainability to build their brand and reputation, while dealmakers structure agreements that capitalize on the financial advantages of green development.

NEGOTIATING GREEN DEALS: A WIN-WIN APPROACH

For dealmakers, sustainability represents a powerful tool in negotiations. Structuring deals that incorporate green development practices can attract investors, reduce costs, and align with market demands.

Strategies for Negotiating Green Deals:

1. **Highlight Cost Savings:** Emphasize the long-term savings from energy efficiency and reduced operational costs.
2. **Leverage Incentives:** Identify government grants, tax credits, or financing options available for green projects.
3. **Align with Investor Values:** Demonstrate how sustainability aligns with investors' goals for risk reduction and future-proofing.
4. **Build Partnerships:** Collaborate with contractors, suppliers, and consultants who specialize in green development.

By positioning sustainability as a mutually beneficial strategy, dealmakers can create agreements that satisfy all parties while advancing environmental goals.

THE ENTREPRENEUR'S ROLE IN GREEN DEVELOPMENT

Entrepreneurs are often at the forefront of innovation in sustainability. Their ability to identify emerging trends and adapt quickly makes them ideal advocates for green development.

Opportunities for Entrepreneurs:

- **Branding:** Build a reputation as a leader in sustainability, attracting eco-conscious customers and investors.
- **Innovation:** Develop new products, services, or business models that address sustainability challenges.
- **Community Engagement:** Partner with local organizations to promote sustainability and gain community support.

Entrepreneurs who embrace sustainability position themselves as forward-thinking leaders, creating a competitive edge in a rapidly evolving market.

DEVELOPERS AND SUSTAINABILITY: TURNING VISION INTO REALITY

For developers, sustainability is about more than meeting market demand, it's about creating projects that stand the test of time. By integrating green practices into every stage of the development process, developers can deliver properties that are efficient, resilient, and profitable.

Key Steps for Developers:

1. **Early Planning:** Incorporate sustainability goals into the project's initial design and budgeting stages.
2. **Collaboration:** Work closely with architects, engineers, and contractors to ensure that green practices are implemented effectively.

3. **Performance Metrics:** Use tools like energy modeling and life-cycle analysis to measure the project's environmental impact.
4. **Marketing:** Highlight the property's green features to attract buyers, tenants, and investors.

Developers who prioritize sustainability not only meet market expectations but also enhance the long-term value of their projects.

REAL ESTATE ECONOMICS AND SUSTAINABILITY

Understanding the economic principles behind sustainability is critical for developers, entrepreneurs, and dealmakers. My book, *Real Estate Economics, Property, Markets, Principles, and Practices*, provides a comprehensive overview of how economic forces shape the real estate market, with a focus on sustainability and green development.

This book offers actionable insights into how sustainability impacts property values, market demand, and investment opportunities. Readers who explore these principles will gain a deeper understanding of how to navigate the complexities of green development and make informed decisions.

Sustainability is not just an ethical imperative, it's an economic opportunity. By mastering the intersection of real estate economics and green development, you can position yourself for success in a rapidly changing industry.

THE ROAD AHEAD

Sustainability and green development are no longer optional, they are the future of property development, entrepreneurship, and dealmaking. By embracing sustainable practices, you can reduce costs, attract investments, and build a reputation as a leader in the real estate market.

This chapter has explored the opportunities and strategies associated with sustainability, from green building practices to negotiating eco-friendly deals.

For a deeper understanding of the economic principles behind sustainability, refer to my book *Real Estate Economics, Property, Markets, Principles, and Practices*. Together, these insights provide a roadmap for navigating the challenges and opportunities of green development.

As you move forward, remember that sustainability is not just a trend, it's a responsibility and an opportunity to shape the future of real estate.

CHAPTER 11: TECHNOLOGY AND INNOVATION IN PROPERTY DEVELOPMENT

Technology and innovation are transforming the property development landscape at an unprecedented pace. The integration of advanced tools and platforms, such as PropTech, artificial intelligence (AI), 3D modeling, virtual reality, and smart building systems, is revolutionizing how developers, entrepreneurs, and dealmakers approach real estate. These technologies not only streamline operations and improve efficiency but also create new opportunities for growth, sustainability, and profitability.

This chapter delves into the role of emerging technologies in property development and how they empower stakeholders to achieve greater success. From identifying prime sites and building sustainable projects to securing financing and closing deals, technology has become an indispensable tool in the real estate industry.

This chapter also serves as a preview of a future book focused entirely on technology and innovation in property development. That book will explore these concepts in greater depth, offering a comprehensive guide to leveraging technology for competitive advantage in real estate. For now, let's explore how these advancements are reshaping the industry.

THE RISE OF PROPTECH: THE FUTURE OF REAL ESTATE

PropTech, short for property technology, refers to the digital innovations transforming the real estate industry. These technologies are designed to streamline processes, enhance decision-making, and create more efficient and transparent transactions. For property developers, entrepreneurs, and dealmakers, PropTech is a game-changer that enables faster, smarter, and more sustainable projects.

Key Applications of PropTech:

1. **Site Analysis and Selection:** Platforms like GIS mapping and AI-powered tools provide detailed insights into site potential, helping developers identify the best locations for projects.
2. **Digital Marketplaces:** Online platforms connect buyers, sellers, landlords, and tenants, simplifying transactions and expanding market reach.
3. **Property Management:** Smart systems automate maintenance, rent collection, and tenant communication, improving efficiency and tenant satisfaction.
4. **Data Analytics:** Advanced analytics tools process large volumes of data to provide actionable insights on market trends, pricing, and demand.

For developers, PropTech enables better decision-making and resource allocation. Entrepreneurs can use PropTech to create innovative business models, while dealmakers rely on it to negotiate deals more effectively and access new markets.

ARTIFICIAL INTELLIGENCE: ENHANCING DECISION-MAKING

Artificial intelligence (AI) is revolutionizing property development by automating complex processes and providing predictive insights. From analyzing market trends to optimizing construction schedules, AI empowers stakeholders to make informed decisions faster and with greater accuracy.

Key Applications of AI in Real Estate:

1. **Market Analysis:** AI algorithms analyze historical data and current trends to predict future market conditions, helping developers and entrepreneurs stay ahead of the curve.
2. **Customer Insights:** AI-powered tools analyze buyer and tenant behavior, enabling personalized marketing strategies.
3. **Construction Optimization:** AI systems schedule tasks, allocate resources, and monitor progress to reduce delays and cost overruns.
4. **Risk Management:** AI models identify potential risks in projects, from financial setbacks to regulatory issues, enabling proactive mitigation.

For developers, AI streamlines project planning and execution. Entrepreneurs use AI to tailor offerings to customer needs, while dealmakers leverage it to evaluate potential investments and structure deals with precision.

3D MODELING AND VIRTUAL REALITY: BRINGING PROJECTS TO LIFE

3D modeling and virtual reality (VR) are transforming how properties are designed, marketed, and experienced. These technologies allow stakeholders to visualize projects in detail before construction begins, enhancing communication, reducing errors, and improving buyer and tenant engagement.

Applications of 3D Modeling and VR:

1. **Design Visualization:** 3D models provide a realistic view of architectural designs, enabling developers to identify potential issues and make adjustments early.
2. **Virtual Tours:** VR allows prospective buyers or tenants to explore properties remotely, saving time and expanding market reach.
3. **Stakeholder Presentations:** Developers can use VR to present project concepts to investors, gaining buy-in and securing funding.
4. **Construction Planning:** Detailed 3D models help contractors and engineers plan workflows and identify potential challenges.

For developers, these technologies improve collaboration with architects, contractors, and stakeholders. Entrepreneurs use VR to enhance marketing efforts and attract customers, while dealmakers utilize 3D models to showcase project value during negotiations.

SMART BUILDING SYSTEMS: THE FUTURE OF PROPERTY MANAGEMENT

Smart building systems integrate technology into the infrastructure of properties, automating processes and enhancing efficiency. These systems include energy management, security, and tenant services, creating buildings that are not only more sustainable but also more appealing to buyers and tenants.

Features of Smart Building Systems:

1. **Energy Efficiency:** Systems that monitor and optimize energy use reduce utility costs and environmental impact.
2. **Automated Maintenance:** Sensors detect issues such as leaks or equipment failures, enabling proactive repairs.
3. **Tenant Experience:** Smart systems offer conveniences like keyless entry, climate control, and personalized settings.
4. **Data Collection:** Smart buildings generate data on usage patterns, providing insights for improving operations.

For developers, smart building systems increase property value and appeal. Entrepreneurs can use these features to differentiate their offerings, while dealmakers highlight the long-term savings and sustainability benefits to attract investors.

THE DEALMAKER'S ADVANTAGE: LEVERAGING TECHNOLOGY IN NEGOTIATIONS

For dealmakers, technology provides powerful tools for structuring and closing real estate transactions. From data-driven insights to enhanced presentations, these tools enable dealmakers to create compelling cases for investment and secure favorable terms.

How Dealmakers Use Technology:

1. **Data Analytics:** Leverage PropTech platforms to present market trends, ROI projections, and risk assessments to stakeholders.
2. **Virtual Presentations:** Use VR and 3D modeling to showcase projects and demonstrate value.
3. **Smart Contracts:** Employ blockchain-based systems for secure, transparent, and efficient transactions.
4. **Negotiation Tools:** AI-powered platforms analyze negotiation dynamics and recommend strategies for achieving optimal outcomes.

By incorporating technology into their processes, dealmakers can enhance transparency, build trust, and close deals more effectively.

THE ENTREPRENEUR'S EDGE: INNOVATING WITH TECHNOLOGY

Entrepreneurs thrive on innovation, and technology provides endless opportunities to create unique value propositions in real estate. From launching PropTech startups to integrating AI and VR into their business models, entrepreneurs can use technology to redefine the industry.

Opportunities for Entrepreneurs:

- **Disruptive Business Models:** Develop platforms or services that address unmet needs in the market, such as co-living or remote property management.
- **Customer Engagement:** Use AI and VR to create personalized, immersive experiences for buyers and tenants.
- **Sustainability Solutions:** Innovate in green building technologies to align with market demand and regulatory requirements.

Entrepreneurs who embrace technology position themselves as leaders in a rapidly evolving industry, gaining a competitive edge and attracting investment.

THE DEVELOPER'S PERSPECTIVE: BUILDING WITH INNOVATION

For developers, technology is a tool for enhancing every stage of the property development process. From site analysis to construction and marketing, innovation enables developers to deliver projects more efficiently and sustainably.

How Developers Use Technology:

- **Site Selection:** Use AI and GIS mapping to identify high-potential sites based on market trends and demographics.
- **Construction Efficiency:** Implement 3D modeling and smart systems to streamline workflows and reduce costs.
- **Market Reach:** Leverage PropTech platforms to connect with buyers and tenants, both locally and globally.

By integrating technology into their projects, developers can achieve better outcomes and create properties that meet the needs of modern consumers. Innovations like smart home systems, energy-efficient designs, and digital management tools not only enhance functionality but also increase property value and appeal.

REAL ESTATE ECONOMICS AND TECHNOLOGY

Technology and innovation are reshaping the economics of real estate. My book, *Real Estate Economics, Property, Markets, Principles, and Practices*, explores how these advancements impact property values, market trends, and investment opportunities.

For those seeking a deeper understanding of the intersection between technology and real estate, this book provides detailed insights into how tools like PropTech and AI influence the industry. By mastering these concepts, developers, entrepreneurs, and dealmakers can make more informed decisions and capitalize on emerging opportunities.

THE ROAD AHEAD

Technology and innovation are not just tools, they are the driving forces shaping the future of property development. From PropTech and AI to 3D modeling and smart building systems, these advancements offer endless possibilities for creating smarter, more efficient, and more sustainable projects.

This chapter has explored how developers, entrepreneurs, and dealmakers can leverage technology to achieve their goals, whether it's identifying prime sites, securing financing, or closing deals.

For a deeper dive into these concepts, stay tuned for my upcoming book on technology and innovation in property development, which will provide a comprehensive guide to navigating the digital transformation of real estate.

As you move forward, remember that technology is not just about staying competitive, it's about redefining what's possible in real estate.

CHAPTER 12: CASE STUDIES IN PROPERTY DEVELOPMENT

Case studies in real estate are invaluable tools for understanding the intricacies of property development, dealmaking, and entrepreneurship. They offer practical, real-world insights into successful projects, allowing stakeholders to learn from proven strategies, overcome challenges, and achieve desired outcomes. Whether you are a developer, entrepreneur, or dealmaker, case studies provide a roadmap for applying theoretical concepts in real-world scenarios.

This chapter presents fictional yet realistic examples designed to illustrate the dynamics of property development. Each case study is tailored to highlight specific lessons, from managing large-scale developments and structuring innovative deals to building entrepreneurial ventures in real estate. By exploring these examples, you will gain a deeper understanding of the challenges, opportunities, and strategies involved in property development.

CASE STUDY 1: THE DEVELOPER'S PERSPECTIVE.
PROJECT: RIVERVIEW RESIDENTIAL COMPLEX

Outcome: A sustainable, high-demand residential project
Key Concepts: Market analysis, planning, and sustainability

Riverview Residential Complex began as an ambitious project to transform a neglected riverside area into a thriving urban community. The developer faced initial challenges, including stringent environmental regulations and limited community support. However, through meticulous market research (as discussed in Chapter 2), the team identified an untapped demand for eco-friendly, affordable housing.

Strategies Employed:

1. **Sustainability as a Selling Point:** The developer embraced green building practices, integrating solar energy systems, rainwater harvesting, and efficient waste management into the project.
2. **Community Engagement:** Regular workshops and consultations were held with local stakeholders to address concerns and build support.
3. **Pre-Selling Units:** Leveraging techniques outlined in Chapter 8, the developer secured early buyers by offering discounted rates and showcasing 3D models of the planned complex.

Lessons Learned:

- Sustainability can be both a regulatory requirement and a marketing advantage.
- Community buy-in is critical for overcoming resistance to large-scale developments.
- Pre-sales can mitigate financial risks and generate early momentum.

This case demonstrates how developers can turn challenges into opportunities by aligning their projects with market demands and community needs.

CASE STUDY 2: THE ENTREPRENEUR'S PERSPECTIVE. PROJECT: CO-WORKING INNOVATION HUB

Outcome: A thriving business model in a competitive market

Key Concepts: Innovation, adaptability, and branding

An entrepreneur identified a growing demand for flexible office spaces among remote workers and startups. The goal was to create a co-working hub that stood out from existing options. However, competition in the sector was fierce, and the entrepreneur faced challenges in securing funding and differentiating the brand.

Strategies Employed:

1. **Targeted Branding:** The hub was marketed as a "community-first workspace," with networking events, workshops, and wellness programs included in membership packages.
2. **Technology Integration:** Smart building systems, such as automated lighting and climate control, enhanced the tenant experience.
3. **Dynamic Pricing Models:** Membership options included hourly, daily, and monthly rates, catering to a diverse clientele.

Lessons Learned:

- Branding is key to creating a unique value proposition in competitive markets.
- Technology can improve tenant satisfaction and operational efficiency.

- Flexibility in pricing and services can attract a broader customer base.

This case highlights how entrepreneurs can innovate and adapt to carve out a niche in the competitive real estate market.

CASE STUDY 3: THE DEALMAKER'S PERSPECTIVE. PROJECT: URBAN MIXED-USE DEVELOPMENT

Outcome: A successful public-private partnership (PPP)
Key Concepts: Negotiation, collaboration, and risk management

A dealmaker was tasked with structuring a complex mixed-use development project in an urban center. The project involved collaboration between private investors, government agencies, and community organizations. Key challenges included balancing stakeholder interests and mitigating financial risks.

Strategies Employed:

1. **Stakeholder Alignment:** The dealmaker facilitated regular meetings to ensure all parties agreed on project goals and deliverables.
2. **Innovative Financing:** A combination of government grants, private equity, and debt financing minimized risks for all stakeholders.
3. **Risk Mitigation:** Contracts included contingency clauses and performance incentives to address potential delays and budget overruns.

Lessons Learned:

- Successful dealmaking requires balancing diverse stakeholder interests.
- Innovative financing structures can unlock opportunities in complex projects.

- Risk management, as discussed in Chapter 10, is essential for maintaining stakeholder confidence.

This case underscores the importance of negotiation and collaboration in dealmaking, particularly for large-scale, high-stakes projects.

INTEGRATING LESSONS FROM CASE STUDIES

Each of these case studies illustrates different aspects of property development, entrepreneurship, and dealmaking. Together, they highlight the importance of innovation, adaptability, and strategic planning in achieving success. Developers, entrepreneurs, and dealmakers can draw on these examples to refine their approaches and navigate challenges with greater confidence.

Key Takeaways:

1. **For Developers:** Align projects with market demands, embrace sustainability, and engage with stakeholders early.
2. **For Entrepreneurs:** Focus on branding, leverage technology, and remain flexible to meet customer needs.
3. **For Dealmakers:** Build strong partnerships, structure innovative deals, and prioritize risk management.

These lessons demonstrate how real-world scenarios can provide actionable insights, helping stakeholders make informed decisions and achieve their goals.

THE ROAD AHEAD

Case studies are more than just examples, they are blueprints for success. By analyzing the strategies and outcomes of real-world projects, developers, entrepreneurs, and dealmakers can identify best practices, avoid common pitfalls, and drive innovation in their own ventures.

This chapter has presented a glimpse into the practical applications of property development, dealmaking, and entrepreneurship. Future books will delve deeper into these case studies, offering expanded insights and additional examples to further empower readers in the real estate industry.

As you move forward, remember that every project is an opportunity to learn, innovate, and succeed. By applying the lessons from these case studies, you can navigate the complexities of property development with confidence and clarity.

CHAPTER 13: CONCLUSION

Real estate is a dynamic realm where the roles of developer, dealmaker, and entrepreneur often intertwine, creating a rich tapestry of challenges and opportunities. These three identities are not distinct but complementary, each contributing unique strengths to the broader narrative of success.

The developer embodies the vision, transforming raw land or neglected spaces into thriving hubs of activity. This process requires more than creativity; it demands relentless problem-solving and the ability to see potential where others see obstacles.

Every structure, from residential complexes to commercial centers, begins as an idea that must be nurtured, refined, and meticulously planned. The dealmaker, on the other hand, is the strategist, navigating the complexities of negotiations, contracts, and partnerships. It is the dealmaker who bridges the gap between vision and reality, forging alliances and securing the resources necessary to bring projects to fruition.

This role demands sharp analytical skills, a deep understanding of financial models, and the ability to build trust in high-stakes environments. The entrepreneur ties these roles together, infusing the process with innovation and a willingness to take calculated risks. Entrepreneurs are the driving force behind disruption, challenging traditional norms and redefining the possibilities of what can be achieved in real estate.

The developer's journey begins with imagination but thrives on execution. Each project presents its own set of constraints, from regulatory hurdles to community concerns.

The ability to overcome these challenges requires not just technical expertise but also the ability to engage with diverse stakeholders. Developers who succeed are those who balance ambition with pragmatism, ensuring that their projects are not only financially viable but also culturally and environmentally sensitive. They understand that real estate is not merely about buildings; it is about creating spaces where people can live, work, and connect.

Meanwhile, the dealmaker operates in a world of numbers and negotiations. This role demands a relentless focus on detail, whether structuring complex financing arrangements or navigating the intricacies of legal agreements. Dealmaking is an art as much as a science, requiring an intuitive grasp of human behavior and an ability to align disparate interests. It is through the dealmaker's efforts that ideas are transformed into tangible ventures, as resources are secured and partnerships solidified.

The entrepreneur, with an eye toward the future, ensures that these efforts remain relevant in a rapidly changing world. Entrepreneurs are not bound by convention; they seek out new markets, leverage emerging technologies, and challenge existing paradigms to deliver innovative solutions. In doing so, they drive growth not only for their businesses but also for the communities and industries they touch.

The interplay of these roles creates a powerful synergy. The developer brings vision, the dealmaker provides strategy, and the entrepreneur ensures adaptability and innovation. Together, they form a cycle of creation and reinvention that defines the real estate industry. Each role feeds into the other, reinforcing the importance of collaboration and the value of diverse perspectives.

Success in real estate is not achieved in isolation but through the careful alignment of skills and ambitions. This interconnectedness is what makes the field so dynamic and rewarding. The stories of the most successful professionals in real estate often reflect this balance, illustrating how vision, strategy, and entrepreneurship can come together to create lasting impact.

The journey of the developer, dealmaker, and entrepreneur is not without its challenges, but it is through these challenges that growth occurs. Each setback is an opportunity to learn, adapt, and refine one's approach. The resilience required in this industry is a testament to the strength of those who choose to engage with it.

Real estate is not for the faint of heart, but for those willing to embrace its complexities, it offers unparalleled rewards. This book has sought to highlight the interconnected roles that drive the industry forward, providing insights and inspiration for anyone seeking to make their mark.

As we close, it is clear that the spirit of the developer, the ingenuity of the dealmaker, and the courage of the entrepreneur will continue to shape the future of real estate, leaving behind legacies of innovation and transformation.

Every real estate developer, dealmaker, and entrepreneur brings unique strengths to the table, but the true magic lies in the ability to combine these skills into a cohesive whole.

If you are one person striving to succeed, it is invaluable to develop a blend of these capabilities, learning to envision projects like a developer, negotiate deals like a dealmaker, and approach challenges with the creativity and risk-taking mindset of an entrepreneur. However, if mastering all three is not feasible, collaboration becomes essential.

A developer who understands the art of dealmaking or works closely with skilled negotiators can unlock greater opportunities, ensuring contracts and partnerships align with long-term goals. Similarly, incorporating an entrepreneurial spirit into development efforts ensures that projects remain innovative, adaptable, and profitable.

For those focused on one role, the key lies in building strategic relationships, developers working alongside dealmakers, dealmakers partnering with visionary entrepreneurs, and entrepreneurs drawing on the expertise of developers to ground their ambitions. Striking this balance and fostering these relationships can yield the greatest benefits in the ever-evolving world of real estate.

I wish you every success in honing your skills, building your expertise, and achieving remarkable results in the real estate market.

Updated List of Books to Date

Willem Tait has authored several insightful books that explore the dynamic and evolving relationship between real estate and capital markets. Each book delves into critical aspects of the industry, offering readers actionable strategies, practical insights, and a deeper understanding of the forces shaping the market. Below is the complete list of books to date:

1. **Real Estate Law Essentials: Navigate Cross-Sections, Avoid Pitfalls, and Seize Opportunities**
   A comprehensive guide to understanding the legal frameworks surrounding real estate, offering practical advice for navigating transactions and mitigating risks.
2. **Proven Principles of Residential Real Estate Investment: Strategies and Tasks for Building Generational Wealth**
   A detailed exploration of residential real estate investment strategies, designed to help readers achieve long-term financial security and success.
3. **Practical Principles of Commercial Real Estate Investment: Tasks and Strategies for Real Estate Success**
   Focused on commercial real estate, this book provides actionable principles and strategies for navigating the complexities of the market and achieving professional growth.
4. **Real Estate Economics: Property Market Principles and Practices**
   This book offers an in-depth analysis of real

estate markets, their underlying principles, and the economic forces driving them.

5. **Raising Money for Real Estate Investment: Close Deals, Raise Money, Build Wealth**
A practical guide to securing funding for real estate projects, this book emphasizes effective deal-making and wealth-building strategies.

6. **Capital Markets and Real Estate: Bridging Markets for a Global Future**
This work explores the intersection of real estate and capital markets, highlighting their convergence and the opportunities that globalization presents for industry professionals.

7. **Real Estate Development and Deal Making: The Essential Guide for Property Developers, Entrepreneurs, and Dealmakers**
This comprehensive guide ties together the foundational principles of property development with innovative strategies for deal-making and entrepreneurship, providing actionable insights for success in the industry.

Real Estate Mastery Books

These books are part of the *Real Estate Mastery Books*, a series designed to equip readers with the tools and knowledge necessary to excel in the fields of real estate and capital markets. This ever-expanding series reflects Willem Tait's commitment to providing actionable insights and strategies. Keep an eye out for upcoming titles in this growing collection, as there are always more exciting additions to come.

ACKNOWLEDGEMENTS

Writing this book has been a journey of learning, collaboration, and inspiration, and it would not have been possible without the contributions of so many incredible individuals.

First and foremost, I want to extend my heartfelt thanks to my readers. Your suggestions and requests for a book on dealmaking and property development were the spark that ignited this project. Your feedback, questions, and encouragement shaped the direction of this work, and for that, I am deeply grateful. Please continue sharing your insights and ideas, your voices guide the stories I tell and the knowledge I share.

To all the professionals who have crossed my path, thank you for your influence on my journey. Architects, quantity surveyors, town planners, building contractors, and project managers, you have each left an indelible mark. Your expertise and dedication have not only inspired but also taught me to see possibilities where others see obstacles.

I want to express my gratitude to my clients, banks, financiers, investors, and partners, those of you on the equity and fee capital sides of the table. Your belief in the vision, your commitment to the process, and your unwavering partnership have been the foundation of so many successful projects. Thank you for walking alongside me, from the moment we looked at a vacant piece of land or an aging building, to seeing what could be rather than what was. Your foresight and courage have challenged me to think bigger and strive harder.

Finally, to every development team I've worked with, thank you for bringing ideas to life. Whether it was a small project or a transformative one, your contributions have been invaluable.

This book is as much yours as it is mine. Thank you all for being a part of this journey, and I look forward to continuing to learn and grow together.

Willem Tait

SOCIAL PROFILES

Willem Tait is committed to staying connected and engaging with his readers. He is active on LinkedIn and X (formerly Twitter), where he shares updates on his latest projects, insights, and resources. Willem is also available for face-to-face consultations, public speaking, and group training sessions through platforms like WhatsApp, Zoom, Google Meet, and Microsoft Teams.

Feel free to reach out on any of these platforms to connect, share ideas, or discuss opportunities for learning and growth. Let's keep building together!

LinkedIn: https://www.linkedin.com/in/willemtait/
X (previously Twitter): https://x.com/willemtait
Calendly: https://calendly.com/willemtait
Email: willemtait@outlook.com

AUTHOR BIO

Willem Tait is an accomplished author, real estate expert, and industry mentor whose journey through the world of property investment, real estate development and capital markets has inspired professionals across the globe. With decades of experience, Willem has become a trusted voice in real estate strategy, capital markets integration, and the transformative power of mentorship.

Willem's passion for education and professional growth is reflected in the six insightful books authored to date. Each work delves into the intricate dynamics of real estate, offering practical strategies, actionable insights, and thought-provoking perspectives on topics ranging from sustainability and innovation to navigating complex financial landscapes. This prolific body of work solidifies Willem's position as an authority in the field, bridging the gap between theory and practice with clarity and expertise.

Beyond writing, Willem Tait holds a strong academic foundation, having pursued advanced studies that inform a nuanced understanding of real estate, economics, and market trends. This dedication to lifelong learning complements a hands-on approach, mentoring aspiring professionals to achieve their goals in real estate and beyond. Known for his ability to break down complex concepts into accessible knowledge, Willem empowers readers and mentees alike to navigate the evolving challenges of the industry.

Whether guiding readers through the intricacies of capital markets or inspiring the next generation of leaders, Willem Tait continues to shape the conversation around real estate and its future. This blend of expertise, passion, and a commitment to growth ensures that Willem remains not just a specialist, but a trailblazer in the ever-changing world of real estate and capital markets.

MENTORSHIP, CONSULTING AND PUBLIC SPEAKING

As a dedicated professional with a passion for real estate, business, law, and economics, I thrive on sharing actionable insights and practical strategies that empower individuals and teams to achieve their goals. My expertise spans real estate investment, business consulting, personal growth, and the intricate connections between legal and economic frameworks, allowing me to offer a well-rounded perspective tailored to diverse challenges and ambitions.

Through public speaking engagements, customised mentorship programs, and dynamic one-on-one or group coaching sessions, I aim to inspire, educate, and guide. Whether addressing an audience of hundreds or working closely with a small team, my mission is to deliver value-driven insights that leave a lasting impact.

If you're seeking a keynote speaker to energise and inform your event, a consultant to elevate your business strategies, or a mentor to foster personal and professional growth, I'm here to collaborate. My approach integrates years of hands-on experience with a solid foundation in real estate, law and economics, ensuring the strategies I share are both practical and informed by robust principles.

Let's connect to explore how I can help you or your organisation unlock new opportunities and achieve meaningful success. Together, we can create strategies that inspire growth, drive innovation, and deliver measurable results.

LinkedIn: https://www.linkedin.com/in/willemtait/

Mail: willemtait@outlook.com

Upcoming Projects

Thank you for joining me on this journey into the fascinating world of real estate. This book is just the first step in what I hope will be a long and meaningful exploration of the strategies, insights, and opportunities that define the real estate landscape.

I'm excited to share that my next book is already well underway. It builds upon the foundation laid here, diving deeper into the complexities of real estate investment, development, and market dynamics. Backed by even more in-depth research and practical case studies, this upcoming work will provide actionable advice and fresh perspectives designed to empower your success in this ever-evolving field.

We Value Your Feedback!

Thank you for taking the time to read *Real Estate Development and Deal Making.* Your insights and experiences with this book mean the world to me, and I would love to hear your thoughts.

If you found the strategies and principles in this book helpful, please consider leaving a review on Amazon or your preferred platform. Your feedback not only helps me improve but also helps other readers discover valuable resources for their commercial real estate journey.

Sharing your thoughts can inspire others to take the next step in their investment journey. Whether it's a quick rating or a detailed review, your voice makes a difference!

Thank you again for your time and trust in this book. Wishing you success in all your real estate ventures!

Portfolio of Books by Willem Tait

For more, kindly see www.amazon.com/author/willemtait

BUSINESS BOOKS

1. **Real Estate Law Essentials:** Navigate Cross-Sections, Avoid Pitfalls, and Seize Opportunities.
2. **Proven Principles of Residential Real Estate Investment:** Strategies and Tasks for Building Generational Wealth.
3. **Practical Principles of Commercial Real Estate Investment:** Tasks and Strategies for Real Estate Success.
4. **Real Estate Economics:** Property Market Principles and Practices.
5. **Raising Money for Real Estate Investment:** Close Deals, Raise Money, Build Wealth.
6. **Capital Markets and Real Estate:** How Money and Capital Shapes the Property Market.
7. **Real Estate Development and Deal Making:** The Essential Guide for Property Developers, Entrepreneurs, and Dealmakers.
8. **Psychology of Residential and Commercial Real Estate:** Master the Psychology Behind Real Estate Success.
9. **Philosophy of Residential and Commercial Real Estate:** Exploring the Intersection of Philosophy, People, Property, Purpose and Spaces.
10. **Economics of Banking and Money:** Insight into Power, Trust, and Change.
11. **The Future of Real Estate:** PropTech, Sustainability and Design

SELF-HELP AND MOTIVATIONAL BOOKS

1. **Sort Your Crap Out:** Own Your Choices, Silence Your Critic. Get Stuff Done
2. **Dammit, Get It Together:** Stop Making Excuses and Start Living the Life You Deserve
3. **Stop Giving a Damn and Start Living:** Cut the Crap. Focus on What Matters. Live Fully
4. **Dammit, It's Your Life:** Own Your Mind, Time, and Choices
5. **Dammit, Stop Being Overwhelmed and Overworked:** Reclaim Your Time, Energy, and Sanity

ANNOTATED AND COMMENTARY

1. **The Way to Wealth** (Annotated): With Motivational Commentary by Willem Tait
2. **The Art Of War:** (Annotated): Proven Modern Strategies for Winning in Business, Leadership, and Life by Willem Tait

www.ingramcontent.com/pod-product-compliance
Lightning Source LLC
Chambersburg PA
CBHW071559220526
45469CB00003B/1060